Love, Justice
and
Freedom

Love, Justice
and
Freedom

NASER KAMALI

CONTENTS

PREFACE

I've been thinking of writing my memoirs for some time, but I had been snowed under with work and problems around it until the outbreak of coronavirus pandemic, which was a great opportunity for me to stay at home for a while without any worries. I started to record my memories. On the other hand, Vicky and Richard would always encourage me to write them down.

Finally, one of our friends, Donya, promised to take the responsibility of writing down those recorded voices, which I knew was going to be a difficult thing to do, as I had recorded all those voices with a Bushehri accent; she had to listen to each part several times to write them down.

Accomplishing this purpose, needed someone to be patient and hardworking, and Donya made it,despite all difficulties on the way. I thank her sincerely because of putting all her efforts into gathering and writing my memories.

I did my best to make the long story short by mainly focusing on the time that I spent in the prison. I had experienced being in ward four and ward one of Adel Abad prison when the majority of prisoners, more than 90 percent of them, were those who had been arrested due to anti-Shah demonstrations, and I also had experienced being imprisoned in ward four of Helali prison, in horrible 1360s(1980s).

I sincerely thank Ahmad S for helping me to make a list of killed people in Bushehr and Ebrahim Avakh and Saeid Pourabdollah. Back in the Shah Dictatorship period, we served our prison sentence together, and I thank all other friends who helped me to make and correct the list of political prisoners of Adel Abad Prison. I also thank Tahmineh warmly, who gave me precious pieces of advice to write well. If any name is missing in those two lists at the end of the book it is due to having no more information.

A BUSHEHRI FATHER AND A BORAZJANI MOTHER

I was born in Lar, which is located in Shiraz Province, a city that has a hot and dry climate, surrounded by mountains. It was separated to two major parts after the well-known Iranian earthquake in 1954. Those two parts are known as the old and the new city.

The new city doesn't have an alley, which has turned that to one of the weirdest cities in both Iran and the Middle East in the urbanized world. My father was born in a rich family and his father was from Dashti. My grandfather fled to the Bushehr Peninsula after a tribal conflict, which led to killing a person (Dashti is about 7534km2, and it is located in the southeast of Bushehr, which includes three major parts, which are called Dashti, Kaki, Shanbe. It has a warm and humid climate, and part of it is mountainous. They speak in Persian, and they have their own specific accent. It has mines of sand, limestone, gypsum, and salt.

Grandfather pursued his career in a pastry shop as the confectionery apprentice; after a while, he became a professional confectioner and started to manage the pastry shop on his own. The owner of the pastry shop had only one daughter; after a while, he consented that Grandfather and his daughter get married. After that, the grandfather became the one who manages the shop thoroughly and changes his surname to Ghannadzade (which means the son of a confectioner), and he starts a great life. As a result, my father found the chance to study and live comfortably.

After my grandfather, my dad inherited all the properties he lost in a commercial transaction. As a result, he was forced to rent a small room in the upstairs of an office located in a terminus, which was close to Saadat school.

This terminus was mainly used by trucks that transported goods between different cities. After working in various fields, he was employed as an accountant at the treasury.

After a while, he was sent to Borazjan due to picking a quarrel with head of the office.

Borazjan is a small, hot city, almost without any facilities and where those who were forced into exile once lived. Borazjan is the second big city of Bushehr province, and Bushehris who want to get to Shiraz and Kazeroon from Bushehr should pass through it. They speak Persian but with a special accent. (The city is famous for its historical palace. Qajari Caravanserai and the political prison of Pahlavis until 1351(1972) which got closed, and afterwards, prisoners were transported to Adel Abad and Shiraz).

Afterwards, my father was forced into exile to I Fasa, another city of the Fars Province.

The city of Fasa is located 135 km east of Shiraz in the Fars Province. Its area is 4302 square kilometres, and its city dates to the Achaemenid Period. It's rather warm and mountainous. He continued his life in exile in Lar; by that time, he had already five children, including three sons and two daughters.

Abdolreza, my father, got married to Masumeh, my mother. My mom was born into a rich family and had two brothers. Her family had lots of gardens and shops so that they were considered as rich people of the city.

My mom's father helped Qazanfar-ol-Saltane financially during war against England.

Qazanfar-ol-Saltane left his properties with my mom's father for safekeeping (Mirza Mohammad Khan Borazjani well-known as Qazanfar-ol-Saltane Borazjani, was philologist, poet, and the governor of Borazjan. He was one of the most effective people of the southern uprising against the British invasion.

One of his important accomplishments was uniting Tangestan fighters and also helping Sheikh Hosein Khan Chah Kuhi and Zaer- Khezr-Khan in their last fight against British forces in Sarbast Choghadak battle.

He was killed by Pahlavi government on the second of Esfand 1308 (February 2, 1930) near Shah-Pesar-Mard-Dashtestan tomb. My mom's father had helped a lot to the Dashtestan uprising.

After my mom's father death, his relatives fought over his properties so that my mom was somehow forced to go to Lar and live with her cousin, which led to her marriage with my dad. She had two children, a girl and boy. My father's dead body was found on a mountain while his second child was only one-and-a-half years. While dad was living in exile, he had some sort of conflict with a group of smugglers due to variety of reasons, including the fact that he was the head of the treasury accounting, and he had to control the financial issues of the city. They would cultivate Poppy at that time. The government had somehow allowed them, and the boss of the treasury was bribed to let them do what they wanted; father couldn't tolerate the situation, and being interested in the Tudeh Party, became a factor to inform the Tudeh Party about the whole thing who were based in Shiraz and those reports were published in the Party newspaper, which was not favourable by the head of treasury and smugglers. The government tries to keep him in exile, and after that, the father starts a series of correspondence in the hope of being transferred to Shiraz, but the government did not agree. Meanwhile, his spleen disease became worse. The doctor of the city wrote a letter to the government, but they didn't care about his health status so he was forced to spend his life with all those difficulties. He made a series of changes to his life. His entertainment become s hunting and regularly going to the mountains by Majlesi motorcycle (big war motorcycle) and tried to get away from the city to calm his nerves.

1337(1959): One day, my father's dead body was found in mountains; he was only 42 years old. My mom was called to go to the hospital to identify the corpse. My mom said his body had completely turned black, and the cause of death was not explained to us. Back then, the head of the Farhang (culture) Department, who was a close friend of my father and was one of the Tudeh party supporters, closed all Lar's schools due to my father's funeral. My sister explained that when she went to the school in the morning, suddenly it was announced that the school was closed, and said it was closed due to my father's funeral.

I was just a kid, and I couldn't truly feel what was going on. I was just happy that school had been closed! There was no one else to investigate his death.

After the revolution, I went to Lar once again as soon as I got the chance to do so. First, due to changing my Deprivation card to the Temporary Exemption of military service card during peace and also to look into his death. The Deprivation Card was given to those who were at least two years in prison during Pahlavi Dynasty, and we were deprived of all social rights for ten years.

After the revolution, the temporary government changed that to the Exemption Card, during peace time.

I got in touch with one of my friends who we had served our prison sentence together in Adel Abad prison, who was originally from Lar.

I asked for his help to clarify the reason for my father's death. He introduced me to the head of the educational system of that time. Despite being so old, he gave me some information, including the location of his cemetery and explained thoroughly about the day of his funeral and that schools had been closed. He believed my father had been killed by the government with support from smugglers, but he was not sure about it. Forensic experts said my father had died either of a snakebite or heart attack, but they found no sign of a snakebite. Surely, he had been killed by the government. I asked him to introduce me to someone who had access to that day's official documents and files. He told me that the doctor died in an earthquake, and he added that I might be able to find some evidence in the gendarmerie. He set an appointment, and I went to the head of the gendarmerie. He greeted me warmly but after asking so many questions, he said that most files and official documents had disappeared during the earthquake of 1339 (1961).

This issue is still a mystery for us. After my dad's death, my mom came back to Borazjan and started to live with his eldest brother in his father's house once again.

After a year, as my stepsister and brother were in Bushehr, and we had already missed them, we immigrated to Bushehr. We used to live on a low income of my mom working as a tailor and my father's pension. My father had another wife, who we would call Nane (Mom); she was so kind. She accepted us. We had rented a room in the Jabri neighbourhood, and we used to live there. In addition to the money that my mom used to earn through working as a tailor, she also inherited some money after her father's death. F ather's pension was also a great help for us to live.

In 1339 (1960), Nane decided to buy a land in Sangi neighbourhood, which was known as Turks' neighbourhood. She also suggested that my mom could buy a land next to hers.

Sangi is an old neighbourhood of Bushehr, which has some mines of stones and clay; most houses had been built by the stones from those mines and clay was used for making the roofs. Turks' neighbourhood was for poor people to live. Most of them had moved from Kooar, which is a small city in the Fars Province. Kooar city is located southeast of Shiraz, 45 km from Shiraz. Its people are so hardworking, but due to problems such as unemployment, they had moved to suburbs of Bushehr. As they had a Turkish accent, that neighbourhood was well known as Turks' neighbourhood. Most worked in mines or the custom's office. It had also so many fertile lands, and some people used to work as farmers and ranchers there as well. They didn't have electricity or purified water. They would bring water in a tin container from a valve in the city for drinking and cooking and a water well for general items.

I was brought up there despite all difficulties, and I had to struggle with all challenges in the way of living! Mom had some jewellery and left it with Abdol-Rasul-Nami for safekeeping, so she built a building on the land with her money, and we moved to Sangi in 1340 (1962).

Back then, I had to wait for six months to enter elementary school, but as my mom was familiar with the head of the school, who was my father's old friend, I was accepted to enter the Saadat School that was manged by Mr Forutan, who was also my dad's friend as well.

This school was built next to Nane's house, so it made me stay more time in Nane's house. My first teacher was Mr Gomrakchi, who was also my dad's friend, and he was so respectful to me until the day that I broke one of my friend's head with a stone. He was the son of a family in the city. Mr Gomrokchi didn't let them expel me from high school under the condition I did not go to that school the following year.

I passed the first year with the best score so my mom sent me to the Mehran School, which was a public one and closer to our home.

Due to some issues, we were made to go back to the previous neighbourhood, Jabri, where we once lived. I registered in the Ferdosi School, and my first teacher was Mr Hoseini. I have good memories of him.

For fourth grade, I was sent to Chahar Aban School. In the beginning, we fought with some guys at the school, so they sent us to a school that was located in the Zolm Abad neighbourhood.

This neighbourhood was one of the poorest and the most violent neighbourhoods of Bushehr. Most people were used to work as fishers or in smuggling goods, not drugs, and some were busy working at ports. Some of them were called Pilevar (Pilevars were those who used to go to Arab countries and would bring goods to sell).

MEHRAN SCHOOL WAS THE STARTING POINT OF STUDYING BOOKS FOR ME

I went to Mehran once again for studying in the fifth and sixth grade of elementary school, which was a turning point in my life as I got to know a person who encouraged me to read various types of books. His name was Mr Khadivar. He and the manager of our school, Mr Ashrafi, played an important role in making me enthusiastic to read almost all the books in our library.

I attended the third important high school of Bushehr, which was close to airport and named Pahlavi (the name of the Iran's kingdom before the revolution). It was a newly-built high school. I became familiar with a totally new situation there. Two people prepared a better situation for us to read more books the first person was Mr. Babachahi (an open minded clerk)who used to teach in the high school and the second person was Mr.Kazemi who was the sports coach of our school; he would take us to the outside of school for exercising while teaching us how to read books properly.

Mr Mohseni, despite being an aggressive literature teacher, was so helpful to students,;more over, he was able to play violin and had already played with many famous singers of his time.

He would talk about the prison atmosphere, and he would put a lot of effort into making students interested in reading books, too.

Mr Aghaei was an amazing teacher. He used to teach both literature and mathematics as well!

One day, I was secretly reading a book by Mickey Spillane while he was teaching geometry. In the blink of an eye, without me noticing, he appeared right next to me and before I had the chance to hide the book, he slapped me in the face angrily and threw the book out the window. He kicked me out of the class, and I stood at a corner not to be seen by the aggressive school manager, Mr Zekavat.

Right after class, the teacher asked me to go into the class. I was shaking in fear, and I approached him and he asked me why I was reading the book so I explained the joy I felt while reading books. He smiled and gave me a book as a gift, which was named Por Malal (meaning full of annoyance) by Amin Faghiri and told me if I liked to read books, go for this one, which was much more worth it. This moment was the most important turning point in my life.

Mr Aghaei used to read books for us in his classes, and he would ask the students to give a summary. I'll never forget when he gave us the Mahie Siah (meaning black fish) book by Samad Behrangi (an author and social activitist who was born in 1318 (1939) in Tabriz and was killed in 1347 (1968) due to an unknown cause) and asked us to give a summary about it. He explained a little bit about the author and his books.

Entering the air force to the city was the beginning of a series of conflicts between ordinary people and the Air Force staff. People couldn't stand their existence and wouldn't let them enter the city due to Bushehr's traditional culture. In 1348 (1969), opening a brothel in the city led to violent conflicts. All people from different neighbourhoods, including the Sangi, Shokri, and Zolmabad neighbourhoods attacked the brothel and set it on fire, so air forces got involved in a big fight with people.

The occurrence led to closing the brothel. We had made an unsafe situation for the air forces. We would hurt them by any possible means, and we would steal their stuff while they were swimming in the sea so that they had to go back home naked. But the air forces changed their strategy, and they started to make a friendly relationships with young people and employed some young people who had the least university degree, and they controlled the chaos.

Typically in summers when schools were closed, Mom would send me to Borazjan City, where my mom's family used to live as it was really hard to control me when the schools were closed, so I was made by my mom to go to Borazjan.

There was a literary political group in Borazjan, which was organised by a person whose name was Rasoul Parvizi; their meetings would be held in Mr Jalali's house.

Rasoul Parvizi was originally from Bushehr and was a member of Tudeh party (The Tudeh Party of Iran is an Iranian communist party formed in 1941, with Soleiman Mirza Eskandari as its head; it had considerable influence in its early years and played an important role during Mohammad Mosaddegh's campaign to nationalize the Anglo-Persian Oil Company and his term as prime minister) in Bushehr, journalis,t and an author who had become one of the Pahlavi's kingdom supporter in the last years of his life;.Shalvarhaie Vasle dar and Gheseie Einakam (meaning the story of my glasses) were some of his famous books.

My mom and some other relatives used to cook lunch and dinner for them, which led me to get familiar with this literary community; he gave me the Shalvarhaie Vasledar book to read.

One of our duties was to distribute election tracts; especially for a specific candidate who was supported by Mr Parvizi.

Mr Ilampour was one of the people that I really liked. He was the husband of my mom's one of the activists against Reza Shah (Iran's king during Pahlavi kingdom) and had been kept in the Falakol Aflak prison for some time and was one of the close friends of Ali Omid. My aunt would compliment him often.

Ali Omid was one of the labour movement activists in Abadan, and he was so close to Yousef Eftekhari who died in 1325 (1973) (Yousef Eftekhari was among the first people who organised the labour movement) in 1349, most of our teachers were living there in exile, exactly the year that Siahkal event affected our society.

Back then, we had a teacher named Mr Abdolhosein Zarifi, who was a member Tudeh Party. In his physics classes, he would introduce books to us as well. He was arrested in 1352 (1973) and spent some time in Abdol Abad prison of Shiraz and after that he went back his home in Abadan. He died in 1356 (1977); his death was so suspicious. Back then, he was a driver of a gas canister company.

Getting familiar with social poems and discussions, some people became rebellion in Jam (it is next to the Fars Province, east and northeast and has a mountainous climate. It is also one of the mountainous areas of Bushehr, which has a pleasant climate).

We would try hard to get more information about the society. That year, we had become so sensitive about social events in our surroundings.

In the fifth grade, we were sent from Dariush Kabir high school to Amirkabir. That was when I met Mr Saeed Ghazian, a political exile teacher. He used to teach literature, but his classes had a totally different atmosphere compare to other classes, which had root in his special attitude towards all events.

Once, when Mr Ghazian was teaching literature history , I interrupted him and asked him a question: "Why don't you talk about other issues? For instance, what's going on in South Africa instead of just talking about literature?" With a nice smile, he wrote on the board, "How did mankind turned to a beast?"

This was the first book he suggested we read and Saeid asked me to stay in the classroom. He spoke so friendly to me and introduced Bid Sorkhi's books and asked me to read these books. By this, he thoroughly changed my studying system (Hamid Momeni, well-known as Bid Sorkhi) was one of the theoreticians of the People's Guerrillas Organisation who died in 1354 (1975) by SAVAK(Pahlavi's intelligence service).

He was teacher and a poet and wrote lots of books about history for teenagers, such as A Brief History of the Society For Teenagers and The Introduction to History.

We started a wall newspaper, which was called Future Open-minded Fedais, and we would use the contents of Jonge Sahar a lot. Until the trial of Khosro Golsorkhi and his co-defendants began, and I chose a poem by Khosrow Golsorkhi for the headline of the wall newspaper and wrote about their trial. But the wall newspaper was removed from the wall quickly, and I was summoned to the high school office. Mr Ghadiri, who was the principal of the high school, closed the wall newspaper with several insults. And he said that I was lucky that he did not inform the authorities. But Mr Kamandi comforted me. In fact, my focus turned to studying more to become more aware of the society situation. I would try to communicate with teachers who were in exile d to get more information about society and gain more experience.

The following summer, I was employed with an Israeli construction company, which led me to get to know the society and labour societies more. Mr Saeid Ghazian also helped me, and I was supposed to give its report after the school's opening. In summer, I went to Shiraz, and I tried to get in touch with university students and I bought lots of books.

Khosro Moeini was another teacher who played an important role to increase our knowledge about society. I learned from him to be serious. Saeid introduced the Patriotic radio station to me, and he gave me a small radio and also had me add newspaper reading to my daily life. As I was student, and I couldn't afford to buy a newspaper, he would give me Keihan newspapers after he read them, and he would mark some articles for me as well. Soon afterwards, we started to do some research on Iran and world history.

We used to read books about Cuba, Palestine, and Vietnam, and I should also mention that I used to take part in religious communities before getting to know political exile teachers. These communities would talk about Quran and discuss about about religious issues. I got to know Dr Shariati's books as well. But religion couldn't answer our curious minds. During the 2500-year celebration of the Persian Empire, as we hated Pahlavi Dynasty without even thinking about the reasons, we would try to break the light bulbs in Tagh Nosrat.

Once a celebration had been held in Khalij club to celebrate the 2500th anniversary. Marzieh and Pouran had been invited to this celebration as well. We went to that place; as soon as the celebration started, we were all ordered from nowhere to attack with stones and all means. The celebration was cancelled, and no one was arrested. We even attacked and disrupted the Garden Party, which was designed to celebrate 2500 years ago. Of course, we did not have a clear political line. We were just sick and tired of everything; we broke lots of light bulbs. Some of its reasons lied behind those religious communities.

Moving to Borazjan, getting to know Mr Rasoul Parvizi and his friends, getting in touch with political exile teachers, doing systematic research on history, and studying in other fields led to getting far from religious communities. That was the beginning of smoking cigarettes and going to public libraries, where we became familiar with various types of communities and Bushehr's libraries, specifically Dad & Alibashi.

Alibashi Library was such a nice place where we could find some rare books as well, which played an important role in our personality development and increasing our knowledge about the society. It had become a hang-out, and my friends, and Mr Ali Bashi would give us books in installments so that we could pay monthly.

DAD Library, was a place for teachers to gather and other open-minded groups. It also gave us the opportunity to access to many other books. Mr Alibashi would behave so kindly to us. We were a group of three people, and we would study. Saeid Ghazian had given us a piece of advice to not get in touch with each other in school. One of our duties was listening to Mihan Parastan (meaning patriots) radio station and applying things that we would learn from it without letting anybody else get to know them.

The last summer that we went to Shiraz and surfed around Shiraz university, we got to know some political issues, and we brought a lot of books from there.

Sixth year: they moved us from Amir Kabir high School to Saadat High School.

The first day that we went to high school, our class was in a far place that had no facilities, so as soon as we went to the class, we understood that it was not a good place to continue our studies, so we consulted with Saeid; he made veiled references and made us understand to show our dissatisfaction and protest against this issue. We shared our decision with our other classmates to show our dissatisfaction with the situation to change it. Some of our classmates had a different point of view; they wanted to finish the high school at all costs to prepare to start their career. But I was determined to change the situation. I was a type of student who almost all students would count on. I would always go to school with jacket, military pants, and military shoes. Many girls and boys would come to me, for getting book; anyway, finally we decided to write a letter to the manager, Mr Mojed of the high school to express our dissatisfaction with the situation.

He was a real dictator, and nobody dared talk with him, but finally, we decided to write a letter on behalf of students and give it to him. I had prepared myself for any kind of consequence from getting expelled to severe punishment and so on.

One of our classmates who had a nice handwriting wrote the letter, and I was the one who was chosen to be in charge of giving the letter to the manager.

On one of our breaks, while I was shaking in fear, I went to Mr Khadivar, who had made me interested in reading books. He was sitting in a room with other teachers.

I knocked on the door with fear, and I had the letter in my hand. Mr Khadivar, said, "Why are you here?"

My hands were trembling with fear, and I said, "I want to give this letter to Mr Majd." He approached me, took the letter, and said, "You can leave here now."

Despite him asking me to leave the office, I stood in my place. Saeid Ghazian being in the room was a sort of encouragement for me.

Without him saying a word, I had a gut feeling that he wanted me to be determined and stay there.

At the same time, Iraj Saghir, who had graduated recently, literature teacher, and who once lived in our neighbourhood, and became the manager of Iran's Cinema Industry after the revolution. As he was entered the room, he took a look at me as if he knew me. He was the director of the Ghalandar Khane show, and he asked me why I was there. I was encouraged and told him that I had brought a letter for Mr Majd that was about being unsatisfied with our new class. He smiled and said okay, continue.

All teachers soon understood that I was not going to move from my place without a specific result. Saeid stared at me with a weird look, which was asking me to stay in my place. Finally, Mr Khadivar gave the letter to Mr Majd.

Majd was sitting at the table just like a typical boss. He read the letter so fast and looked at me through his glasses and stood.

I was thinking to runaway, but something deep inside had me stay in place. Majd approached me and asked, "What is this," and I explained for him.

He said in a threatening tone, "Go, I don't want to see you again." I stammered and explained that it was not a good place for the sixth literary and wanted to change our place. I just was not beaten and came out of the office and maybe he threw me out of the office with his angry look.

In the afternoon, I met Saeid. After talking for a while, I asked him what should I do. He said when we were in Mashhad, we would protest and show our dissatisfaction more seriously, not just in a letter.

Tomorrow, to the class, I suggested that we protest the following day when standing in line in the morning,and as usual, some of our classmates were against this idea.

The following day in the morning, lines of students went to their classes one after another except us. We were the last line. When Majd came across this situation, he was kindda shocked and understood that this issue was getting serious. For a while, no one talked; neither us nor him. After some seconds, one of our classmates said we are not okay with our class so we wanted to change that. We could expect anything except when Majd said okay, go to your class for now. I will change it in the afternoon.

We couldn't believe what we were hearing. He changed our class, and we went to a class that was next to manager's room.

That was almost the first big point that we got from Majd that no one would expect.

Since then, our classes turned to be a place for social discussions more than a normal class of just studying. Meanwhile, some teachers would enter our discussion as well while the others were against these types of discussions, and they would not let us continue.

We would talk about a variety of subjects from Palestine, Vietnam, and Cuba to prepare for more serious discussions in the future.

We used to listen to Mihan Parastan radio station and take notes of the main points. After a while, we decided to change something about open-minded communities in those days, who wouldn't do anything, just talk and talk and talk.

Those communities, open-minded ones, would always gather in Shemshad Café and get drunk, which was really hard for us to tolerate as in our neighbourhood, KaparAbad, most people were poor immigrants who had come from villages to Bushehr and lost their farms and other property. They mostly worked in boats or as workers to move heavy things from one place to another.

This disparity in wealth was so tangible and annoying, so I had gotten to a point that I knew I ahd to do something about it.

One day, I wrote and read an essay in one of our classes that ended with a poem from Forough Farokhzad in which she had said, "A person will come that will share everything even…"

Though our teacher didn't like it, Mr Irani, the one who always used to wear military clothes, had introduced Ferdosi magazines to us that we really liked would go through them as well.

Generally, we were sick and tired of the entire situation in a country which Shah (The King) was the main reason for the situation.

Following this situation, we made a decision to do some actions against the government, including writing political slogans on city walls and setting some cars that belonged to Savak(the intelligence service of Pahlavi's period) on fire.

We found the best locations to start writing political slogans without anybody becoming aware, even Saeid.

We were a small group of three friends who wouldn't get in touch in school to let anybody become suspicious about the whole thing. We chose some particular slogans. The first slogan, death to Shah, viva communist, and viva Castro , and we started to take action in Azar (9th month of Persian calendar).

My friend who had lovely handwriting would write the slogans, and I would take the paint and brush and the last one of us was responsible for checking the slogans in the final step.

We started from Pahlavi High School and continued our way to the heart of the city. We wrote those slogans in almost every corner of town till morning

The following day in school, we talked with each other about what we did, and we were kindda proud of what we had done; we were just waiting curiously to see people's reaction.

That day, I also met Saeid Ghazian; however, he didn't know anything about what we had done, but out of curiosity, he asked me was us who did that last night.

I said no! Saied gave me a gentle smile and said he wishes nothing bad happens.

I went back to class that day unlike other days. I was so quiet in the class, and in the afternoon, I went to the beach. One of my friends in our group came. We started to walk along the beach and talk about everything around our new journey and our upcoming plans, which included setting a Land Rover of SAVAK on fire. Actually, we expected more reactions, but everything seemed normal, at least seemed normal! I went back home.

The following day, I went to school everything was like before. I saw Saied, who again gave me a gentle smile once again and went to the class.

At Yalda night (the longest night in Persian calendar which is at the end of the azar,9th month of Persian calendar) we gathered once again and started to plan future events.

The following morning at school, I was asked to meet Mr Majd(manager of the school) Majd asked why I was absent.

I wasn't absent; I was always present in class.

"No, you were absent! You should make a commitment to not be absent once again, and if you do so, you will be fired from the school."

I did what I was asked, wondering what was going on. I was scared and thinking about running away from the school; after a while, I was asked to go to the manager's room once again. I felt something was cooking!

Students were looking at me in a weird way. We all had felt something was wrong, but each from his own point of view!

As I entered the room, I saw Majd and Kadivar sitting behind their desk and two persons were standing. I couldn't even get a chance to start to talk before he mentioned "It's him", and those two muscular persons caught me and took me with them; meanwhile, I was looking at them shocked and asking Majd to stop them. Everything happened in a blink of an eye, at least to me! They took me out of the school. There were five or six other angry people waiting for me. Without saying a word, they started to hit me in the worst way that I had ever experienced.

People were watching.

They slapped my face so hard and asked me to show them the way to my home. They had two cars: a Peugeot and a Peikan.

On the way, one of them told me look around because it was my last chance to see the scenes in my life. When I arrived home, my mom started to scream, wodering why her beloved son was carried by some cruel people angrily. They went straight to my room, searching everywhere. They found some books and Shah's picture, which I had drawn a cross line on. After searching the home, they took me to their car, sitting in the back seat between two muscular persons. After a while, a turkish man punched my side in a way that for some seconds felt like I was about to die!

We went to Savak (intelligence service ofpahlavi's kingdom).

Savak had rented an old house on the beach. We went in, they locked the door, and pushed me into a room.

It was a normal with a sofa and a wooden table and nothing else.

After some minutes, the man with Turkish accent came in made me sit on the sofa and stood right in front of me telling me to tell the truth when asked questions; otherwise; I wouldn't even imagine what could happen to me. He punched and slapped me and then left the room.

After a while, he came to the room once again with one his friends and started to humiliate me by making fun of my age and looks.

The man again slapped and punched me; his friend told him there was no need to torture me. I would tell them everything, and if I didn't tell the truth for one per cent, he knew how to make me talk! They left.

A short man came in and started advising me to tell them everything. I still had no idea of what was going on because nobody except us three knew anything about the whole thing!

A person whose name was Mr Mahmoudi came in the room He was the interrogator and originally from Tabriz, and asked me to tell the truth. He said he would be back with a paper and pen to write my confessions, and still, they hadn't asked any questions of the political slogans.

After that, Irvani and Mahmoudi came together and took my hand and dragged me to the second floor to the room of Nasser Salimipour, the head of SAVAK. It was a large room and the head of SAVAK was at the end of the room behind a big desk. We three sat on the seats close to the door; he asked me to approach him. I stood and went in front of his desk. He said sarcastically, "Do you know where is here?"

I said, "Yes, SAVAK."

He said. "Do you know how we torture boiled eggs or Pepsi?"

Khosro Golsorkhi confessed soon after entering. "You are not one hundred percent patient like him. So tell us whatever you know, and do not make us angry either." He said to go. We went to the same room we were earlier. They closed the door and left. I was alone. After some minutes, Mahmoudi said he knew who I was and began the interrogation. I said that I do not know at all, and I'm a student. "You have got me wrong."

The interrogator, without saying anyting, stood and left.

After a while, two people entered with a whip. They laid me down on the floor and took one of my legs, and the interrogator put his foot on my chest, and the other one started to whip. After that, they left the room, and the interrogator and I were left alone. I shouted a lot because I was hurt badly. He started to ask me several questions, but I tried not to say anything. But again, he slapped my face.

He said again that I wrote the slogans at those hours, and he knew who I was. Do you want to be tortured or do you say it yourself ? I started crying and said that they have got me wrong. I do not know what they are saying. It was about 3.5 o'clock when a man came into the room who I had not seen. SAVAK told the interrogator to go out, and he started to comfort me and asked me if I had eaten anything? I cried and said no! He asked what I wanted, and I said I wasn't hungry. He said he would order a food from the Cheshmak restaurant for me. I thought he was making fun of me.

Then he asked what kind of drink I wanted. Small or large? At that moment, I was thinking in my mind that the smaller one was less pain. So I ordered a small according to the mentality that I had from SAVAK. Earlier, in a meeting with the head of SAVAK, he said that they torture by Pepsi.

The interrogation started, and he said, "Now tell me, who did you write those slogans with?" By that time, they were sure the slogans were written by me and my friends. I kept saying no until the moment those two people came in once again and t started to hit me in an awful way. Finally, I admitted we had written the slogans, and I was forced to tell them about those who were with me, and the interrogation was stopped. They brought chelokbab and soda.As I was eating, I heard one of my friend's voices shouting as he was being tortured. They took me to another room next to the toilet. The door was locked, and I looked out of its tiny keyhole. I saw the cell of one of the prisoners who was there and he was beaten and the interrogation continued until midnight. And then they took we three into the first room and gave us blankets to sleep on. We were still shocked by what happened. How were we exposed? The following day, they brought a warrant for our arrest. We were arrested on Dey 13, 1353 (January 4, 1974) for writing slogans against the Shah.

I WAS TRANSFERRED TO BUSHEHR CENTRAL PRISON

A fter a week, the first person was sent to prison, and after 10 days, the second person, and after 14 days, I was sent to Central Bushehr Prison. I got on the Land Rover of SAVAK. I knew his driver who used to live in our neighbourhood. He took a look at me and said, "Aren't you ashamed? Did you want to set our car on fire?" I was your neighbour; and we went to prison. The second floor of the prison was the prison's office, and they took me to the second floor They handed me over to the prison guards. A young officer was standing and said that another saboteur had been brought. Those who assassinated Taheri. And he began to explain that General Taheri was assassinated (General Taheri, a high-ranking police officer who was assassinated by Mohammad Mofidi and Mohammad Baqer).

Okay, kill us; we will kill you too. And in the presence of SAVAK agents, I was slapped on my ear two or three times and said that these saboteurs are the ones who assassinated our brave and patriotic people of Iran, and they took my fingerprints.

They sent me to the first floor while beating me and tied a handcuff and put me behind the guard's office. The cell was a small room where two of my friends were there as well. As soon as we met each other once again, we started to laugh and were happy. Bushehr Prison used to pay prisoners 22 rials, and we got to know Muhammad and shared our expenses with him. He had been arrested because of a fight with one of the naval forces that had led to the soldier's death.

He was also the husband of one of my friend's sister's, One interesting point was meeting Jam Variz.

We were allowed to go to the yard one hour per day, and some days, we got free of the handcuffs as well. However, gradually we were given more free time to go to the yard but still we were not allowed to get in touch with ordinary prisoners; those prisoners used to behave so respectfully towards us. In the afternoons, we had to stamp our name to receive our quota of the money from the prison guard. We didn't accept as we believed that as a part of an educated society we could sign instead of that. Prison guards didn't want to accept that in the first place so, they started to threaten us to act as others, but we were not going to do so. Finally, one of the prisoners did on behalf of us by his toe, an action that prison guards didn't find respectful, so they started to hit him as a punishment and separated him from others till morning.

The following day, they had made a new list, so we were the ones who got to their goals in this particular case.

Normal prisoners had become happy, and they showed us their satisfaction by giving us a broad smile. The prison included various groups of people, including those who were arrested for local fights, smugglers who had smuggled some stuff from Arab countries to Iran, and also few people were prisoned there due to drug and a rebellion whose case was in common with two or three other people as well. Mohammad and also a Kurdish guy who was so...

Bushehr prison was an old building which had two floors and had been rented by Shahrbani (police office in Pahlavi). The first floor had six rooms and there was an old, small bathroom next to it and some toilets as well.

Prisoners were separated into specific groups based on different items from their type of crime to their city and an exercise yard in which most prisoners used to gather and would exercise and talk as well.

Each room was decorated based on the prisoner living there. Despite all other prisoners, we were prisoned in a small cell, and we were only allowed to go to the yard for one hour, and we had to stay in that small cell for the whole day so made complaints, but no one cared. Typically, we had bread, apple, and tea for our breakfast, and for lunches, we mostly had a local food of Bushehr. The bathroom was a small room that had a lamp, and we had to warm up water via that to mix it with cold water to take a bath. We were allowed to take shower only once a week; of course if we could afford buying more oil there was no limitations to taking a bath more.

We would spend our time by talking about various topics and remembering the books that we'd read by then. And sometimes, we were lucky to get access to some sports or weekly magazines that had been left on the table by prison guards. We never asked for a book or newspaper. Maybe we were afraid of

asking them for a book because we didn't have a good experience reading books, well, books that we had gone through had already played an important role in the things that we were involved with.

After some days, they took us to a small dark cell next to the visiting room, which was a small one. A prison guard was always there, and each person had ten minutes to visit his family members or others who had come to visit.

The new place was really a disgusting,but we were happy as a group and generally other prisoners had good feelings about us especially after us being able to make the prison guards change their list. We were gradually feeling that things were serious, and we were believing that we had to stay in prison for a long time. Prison guards would come to us when they were free, and they would tell stories about when the prison was full of Tudeis, and they were sent from here to Khark Island. One guard who was our neighbour and knew us completely was well known as Hosein Sibil (Sibil means mustache in English) as he had a big mustache; he always did his best to prepare a good situation for us. He would also tell a story about a night when many gentlemen wearing suits and ties were taken to the prison as prisoners who were all part of a Tudeh Party, and they didn't need share of the money that was given to prisoners as they were rich. He said after some days, all of them were sent to Khark Island. Due to being in touch with Hosein Shahrestani, our prison guard, who was our neighbour as well, I had the chance to learn that my mom was aware of our situation thoroughly and at some point, he would take us some stuff such as fruit, food, and my mom cookies as well.

There was a prison guard whose name was Jamali. He was always so violent and rude. He would always say if I was allowed to choose something for my destiny, he would send all of us to farms to work as a cow. This became a joke among us. Sometimes, we would put him on as well, and he would find out that we were making fun of him, and he would become so angry. Hosein Shahrestani never allowed him to resort to violence.

Even sometimes prison guards would put him on to have fun. They said that they should also spend our time in a way; they would say that we prisoners would leave after some time but they had to stay forever like a real prisoner.

All people would be freed one after another while it seemed like we were going to stay forever. Day by day, the depth of the disaster was becoming more tangible for us. We attempted several times to get in touch with a quiet rebel in another cell to get to know him more, and the reason that he was in prison. He was not eager at all to talk with others.

Mohammad who had come from Shiraz Prison to Bushehr would always tell us about that prison. He'd emphasize that they would take us to that prison after some time for sure; it was a place for keeping political prisoners.

We spent days and nights until a day I was asked to go to the manager's room. When I entered the room, I saw that two plain-clothed men were waiting for me. The Land Rover driver that we had planned to set his car on fire was there as well; he said we met each other once again while he was smiling.

The prison guard came and gave me a piece of paper and asked me to sign the paper and handed it to those two people. They put handcuffs on me; we got on the Land Rover, and we went to SAVAK.

They were totally quiet, and I didn't know what was going on at all.

We went to SAVAK. They took me into the room that I had been tortured in, the first day I was arrested, and locked the door; it didn't take a long for Iravani to come in, and after greeting me, he asked about the prison situation and stuff around that. He asked if I wanted to be tortured again and did you tell everything.

I asked what was happening. "You know I was in prison!"

He said, "Guess which political communities are still actively after you?"

I said I didn't really know!

He said, "Some political slogans have been written on the sports stadium, and for sure you know those who have done that."

I asked how I would know because I was in prison all these days.

He asked me to guess who was behind it all. I said I didn't know. Suddenly, he punched and kicked me and told me to think carefully. When he returned, maybe I would remember something.

For a while, I was alone in the room and the tall, fat man with Turkish accent came in and said sarcastically, "Oh, you are here once again!"

This time, I knew how to treat you well,and soon afterwards, four other men came in. I was totally scared, but they just wanted to scare me, and after few slaps, they left the room. Mahmoudi, the interrogator, came and started to interrogate me.

He asked similar questions and wanted me to tell them about the identity of those who had written the slogans. I wrote that I didn't know and signed the paper; then he asked me to write about some people I knew, and I wrote about some of our naughty classmates. Mahmoudi then packed his stuff and went out.

I was hell happy that finally our primary movement was showing its result, and it had least led to some similar movements in our city.

I was there until 5 p.m., then I was handcuffed and sent back to the prison once again. As soon as we got to the prison, unfortunately, the same young guard was in the office again. When he saw me, he said "Dirty saboteur, finally I will shoot the last bullet into your head." SAVAKIS handed me to the gurard, and they left. The young officer started to talk angrily, saying I knew that some of the best people of our country have been assassinated by rebels like me. That was our last meeting. After some days, early in the morning, they woke us and asked us to pack our stuff as they were going to send us to another prison in Shiraz. So we did the same and said goodbye to other prisoners. We went to the second floor where six soldiers and a sergeant were waiting for us. Three soldiers were armed, and the sergeant had a colt, but the other soldiers were not armed. After signing the papers, they handed us over to the sergeant who said we are allowed to shoot at you if necessary, so don't think about doing something silly. We were tied up by another soldier and moved. When we came out of prison, I saw my mother waiting. I laughed, but my mother was crying and said they wanted to take me to Shiraz. She had brought some money, cigarettes, and fruits for me and said my uncle said that they were taking me to Shiraz Prison. Back then, he worked in gendarmerie. We were taken to the Mihan car garage on foot. On the way, we saw lots of our friends. We laughed and joked and said goodbye to each other until we got to the bus.

Passengers would look at us in a meaningful way. We got on the bus with the normal passengers. The sergeant said that we were not allowed to talk to anybody.

Bach then, there was a harsh cliff road between Bushehr and Shiraz, which at some points passengers had to get off the bus as it was dangerous to pass some narrow parts that a car could pass, but we had to stay on the bus despite its dangers. Halfway, the bus stopped next to a restaurant that was not clean at all; when I wanted to go to the toilet, the soldier wasn't willing to open the handcuffs so I sat on the toilet while being connect to him with one hand, which was an interesting memory for me.

After having lunch, we got on the bus and went to Shiraz. This time, due to the sergeant's order, both hands were handcuffed to each other and not to the soldiers' hands anymore. Bushehr was 300 km far from Shiraz; it took around seven hours to get there. It was around 7 p.m. when we got to Shiraz. They rented a pickup truck to take us to the prison, which was located in Adel Abad, an inhabited place far from the city; nobody dared going after the dark.

Adel Abad prison was built in 1350 (1971) in the south of Shiraz, and nobody would live around there. It was built similar to American prisons, and there were rumours that Farah Pahlavi had opened it. By the time we got to the prison, it was late night so that the prison guard wouldn't accept us and asked us to come back early the next morning. We were happy as we thought that we were going to stay in a hotel for the night. We stayed there around an hour until they were finally convinced to accept us. The sergeant came to us and said he was sorry for having handcuff us. He was simply carrying out orders.

We entered through the big door of the prison and entered an area that we had no information about it. We each had a bag and a package. The prison guard said sarcastically, "Do you need to listen to a story before sleeping, you little boys". We were taken to the prison warehouse office, which was next to the kitchen. They gave us a black leather slipper and a blue prison uniform, and we headed towards the cells. That was when we started to notice how big and great the prison was; to the left, there were stairs, and to the right, there was a library and a hall. On the left side of the kitchen, next to the stairs, there was an iron door that we entered through. We first passed solitary confinement, which was covered by a curtain so no one could see its inside. Another prison guard took us, and we headed straight to the main cell. There were some guards there; they looked at us carefully and wrote our names on their list. We were guided to our cells without any disrespect. Each of us in a separated cell and they closed the door. This prison had three floors, and all cells were locked with iron doors that had a hole to get food through. They didn't ask if we had eaten. They said we needed anything to let them know by exiting our hands from the cell; then they will come.

There was a bed and two blankets in the cell. The first thing that attracted my attention was a small window without any glass that let cold air come in. It was dark. Right in front of my cell there was another prisoner who looked at me, smiled, and said, "Have you gone on a strike?"

I said no! "We have come from Bushehr."

He said, "I'm a university student. I was arrested because of going on a strike."

That was the first time I saw a political prisoner, so it was good news that we were not alone!

He said it was full of university students and added that tomorrow morning they will open the cell doors, and we will all go to exercise yard.

He asked if I had anything for dinner. I said no, just a lunch on the way, which was awful.

He signaled the prison guard with his hand as he had mentioned to call the guard. When the guard came, he said we new prisoners had nothing for dinner and were hungry. The guard said kitchen was now closed so they cannot prepare food. The young guy said if you open the cells, we have got some leftover food that we can share with them. The guard accepted and gave us some bread and cheese and said that's the only thing left for now. We would get breakfast in the morning, and he gave me a gentle smile. That was the first respectful behaviour we came across in that prison.

After having dinner, I asked them to let me go to the toilet and also to brush my teeth. When I went to the toilet, I found out that everything was different in that prison as all things were clean. It was totally different with Bushehr Prison. I slept till morning with the two blankets, shaking from the cold because as a person who was brought up in Bushehr, which is a hot city, I was not used to living in cold weather at all. Early in the morning, they gave us breakfast and hot tea, which was so enjoyable following the cold night.

Cells doors were opened for all; we were supposed to go to the exercise yard. They told us to get ready as we were supposed to introduce ourselves to the head of the prison, Mr Ghahremani and Adibpour. All prisoners stood in line. Ghahremani, who always had a wooden bar in his hand, came, and Adibpour followed. They asked everyone their first name and surname and their crime until they got to us. Adibpur said sarcastically,"Oh, we didn't know that this prison recently became a kindergarten for kids as well." After that, we were returned to our cells.

Solitary confinement was a place to keep normal political prisoners. They would also bring dangerous prisoners here. There was a prisoner who would always act crazy to persuade them not to execute him. He would sing loud from morning till night, and guards would always treat him in the worst possible way. There were even some people who would say that crazy sometimes piss in his cell as well and the guards would make him eat his own stool.

I never saw such a scene, but the guards could do anything that they wanted, and as time went by, we started to get to know eveyone and become familiar with the atmosphere as well.

Once in the yard, a man came to me and said that he was a university student of Shiraz, and he was originally a Turk from Tabriz. We walked together and talked about the reasons we were arrested. It was then I understood that our case was not something serious compared to other crime cases; getting to know him was the beginning of a new path for us to learn more. Mr Haeri, a tall clerk who became Shiraz Imam Jome(a high rank clerk who holds praying events on Fridays) after the revoloution, was also there. He would always talk alone. Dr Fartouk, who became the head of Shiraz University, was also kept in the prison and would teach Quran, and there was a group of people who would gather and talk about political and economic issues, and they would always exercise in the morning. Ali Dadgar would teach Turkish, and he believed that we had to read Samad (a famous book in 1970 among Iranians) in its original language, and we all would attend his class.

One day when I was walking in the yard, someone put a small piece of paper in my hand and left. I saw that he was an old skinny man that I had never noticed. I went to the toilet and opened it. He had written that tonight was the time of uprising, and with the movement of his hand, we all needed to shout to show our power.

It was also written on the paper that after reading it, give it to someone I trust.

I folded the paper and gave it to Ali Dadgar and told him the story behind it.

He quickly grabbed the paper and tore it up and said that we had to be very careful.

We would spend most of time exercising, studying, and playing games. One night, one of the guards informed us that we had trial the following day and had to be prepared early in the morning. Ali came and said not to worry, It was just an interrogation. "They are gonna start to go through your crime case; maybe you will be released."

Early in the morning, we ate the breakfast and put on our blue prison uniforms and headed out. We stood in line, and Adibpour c took a look at us and left. We signed a paper to leave and were handcuffed. Outside, eight police officers were waiting. Each read a prisoner's name, and we were handcuffed to them. We went towards a minibus that had a lattice window and outside was not visible from the inside. They closed the doors, and we couldn't even see out from the window in front of us. They said we three should go to military court. Back in those days, political prisoners would be always sent to military court. The public prosecutor and all other members were there.

We entered through the prison's big door; it was quite a short distance between the prison and military court, which means the third military.

We entered the court and sat on the seats while our hands were handcuffed to the guards. One of the guards told his friend he hoped our cases were finished soon so that they can get home sooner. Another one said he was awake the previous night, and we figured these guards were tired.

They called my name, and I went to the prosecutor's room. He told the guards while he was gently smiling, "Open his handcuff. I'll call you in when we are done".

They asked me to introduce myself thoroughly, then read my crime case details aloud; it was full of weird things. Of course, I didn't accept the serious items, but I didn't deny that we wrote those slogans and explained our reasons. He laughed and said, "Our king has great plans for our country's future; you are still so young why were you deceived so easily?"

He started to ask several other questions, then told me to wait for a lawyer. He called the guard, and again, I was handcuffed, and we went back. I waited for my friends, and after, we all went back to prison. We signed the paper for entering, and we went to our cells. Ali came and asked what happened. I told him all that happened, and he said it was okay and just the normal process. They would give us a Taskhiri lawyer and explained a bit about it. The Taskhiri lawyer was the one who was chosen by the military court, and he would do his job without asking for money. There was also another type of lawyer called a TAEINI lawyer. He was a lawyer who could be chosen among other lawyers of the family court, and you paid him on your own.

Our life got back to its routine. After some days, my mom came to the prison to visit me. This time, I could see her clearly sitting behind a glass window, and we had to talk through a specific type of telephone, which was there for visitors and prisoners. She said she was trying to find a good lawyer. I said there is no need to do so and waste her money because these lawyers can do nothing special in our case. That was our first visit at prison.

In the following years, when I was released, my mom told me the story of our first visit in the prison from her point of view.

She said she was looking for a way to come to Adel Abad Prison, but couldn't find anyone to take her until a man who found out that I was prisoned due to a political crime and it was our first visit agreed to take her for free, and he even said he would wait for her. As soon as she entered the prison, the guard told her I had been arrested due to a political crime. First, she needed to ask for official permission from SAVAK, and she was saddened and wished I had been arrested for some other reason, like drug trafficking, murder, or even robbery so she could meet with me easily. The guard said she should be proud that I was arrested due political issues. "Our people are proud of people like him." That was when she felt proud of being mom to such a boy.

When she went back to the waiting man, she said she had to go to SAVAK to ask for official permission to visit me. He said it's on Zand Street, but it's closed. He asked her where she wanted to stay, and she said with a relative. He took her there for free.

My mom said that was the first time that she was really proud because she understood that political prisoners were so respectful in ordinary people's eyes. The next morning, she went to SAVAK on Zand Street.

They said it's acceptable to meet him, and to ask the prison for an appropriate time. She didn't get a lawyer as she thought it was useless.

After a while, once again, I was sent to the court to get to know the lawyer who was recommended by the court.

There was on old man in his early sixties who had been retired from the military. We chose him and then went back to the prison. Back in those days, I started to feel like that I had grown up, and I learned how to discuss political issues. Saeid had taught me how to read a newspaper in the correct way, but here, the studying style was totally different.

Dr Fartoukzade had put all his effort into making us interested in religious stuff and attract our attention to him. The conflict between religious people and left-wing politics was crystal clear. Prison was like a university to us, and we started to learn many new things in ward number four. All things were new and interesting. I saw the first snow in ward one. As a person who had been brought up in hot climates, it was the first time that I was seeing snow in my life; of course, I had seen snow in some movies but not in the real life.

Prisoners ordered grape syrup to mix it with snow and eat, which could lead to pneumonia in some cases. Anyway, we experienced our first snow. In ward one, there were ordinary prisoners who were not allowed to visit anyone from the outside and also some drug dealers who were possibly going to be executed. We would prefer just to be in touch with political prisoners, and not others. One day, a new prisoner was brought to the prison. He seemed an imposing man who was a member of People's Mojahedin Organization of Iran; they said he was sick and tired of everything and that he couldn't even tolerate his prison sentence. That was when we were scared that we might end up in a situation like his. Finally, they took us to ward four; we were all happy as we could finally be in a place with all other important political prisoners. As soon as we entered, we started to look at our surroundings curiously. Anyways, they wrote down our names and took us to the second floor, which was in front of the reformatory.

We wondered why didn't take us to the first floor. All days and nights we would watch the teenagers, and gradually, we got to know them.

Ward four had three floors for reformatory, women and political prisoners. We were on the second floor for one week. The only interesting point during that week was getting to know an Iraqi intelligence agent whose name was ALJABOURI, who was on the second floor as well and we used to talk a lot with him. He was replaced by an Iranian in 1957.

In reformatory, most teenagers were there due to stealing; one thing that was nice about them was that they were totally carefree. Every now and then, they would start to dance or sing without any reason. They were kept in ward four to stay safe.

After going to ward four once again, they wrote down our names and sent each of us to a specific room. After the big 1352 (1973) strike in Adel Abad Prison, nobody was allowed to choose his room. In the first month of 1352, political prisoners got control of ward four for two days, which was met with violence from police and led to many people from both sides being injured, including the high-rank person from SAVAK who was Mr Fakhraii.

I was sent to room number 15. When I entered the room, some prisoners welcomed me to the cell and others didn't care that much. This room was dedicated to members of Tudeh Party of Iran. Honestly, in the first place, I was shocked as we knew them as betrayers, so I didn't feel well about it. Before that, I was wishing to be in a same room with members of the Organization of Iranian People's Fedai Guerrillas and to get to know them. Mr Taghi Keimanesh welcomed me in a very friendly way to room 15. Mr Hejri, who was a tall man, stood, shook hands, and introduced himself. I said with lots of excitement that I knew him very well. Soon afterwards, Mr Ali Amooii also said that so he would't introduce himself because I knew him. That was really a good, and I got positive vibes from those people in the room.

After that, I went around the cell and said hello to all those who I came across them. The first room I was invited in was room 21.

Those great days, Alireza Shokouhi, Parviz Jahanbakhsh, Nouri Riahi, Amir Lashkari, Dr Ahmadi, Dr Taghi Afshani, and Javad Oskouii were in the room, and they welcomed me with a glass of tea. That was a great memory for me.

After greetings, one by one, they started to go to their bed I have really missed Ali Shokouhi. They talked with me until the last moment, and I thanked them and left the room.

Mahmoud Mahmoodi, that brilliant guy that I never forget, saw me and said to go to him.

I went to room three, in which Ebad Ahmadzade was also being kept, and Mahmoud told me of his memories back in Bushehr. He called me Shir Mohammad, who was one the characters of Tangsir Choobak book. We talked for a while, and we drank a glass of tea together, and after that, I came out. Bahram Ghobadi, who had been shot by SAVAK, his brother, and also his brother-in-law had been killed by police (and also Mehrnoush Ebrahimi and Changiz Ghobadi). He was shot in his abdomen, Partoi was on his leg, Changiz and Mehrnoush had run away. Bahram was a tall man and had an impressive look. We talked for a while, and he asked me some questions about my studies and my job. I didn't like it that much, but until the last days of prison, I got to talk with him again at some point.

Hasan Saadati was a shy man. We talked for a short time. He was a member of the Toofan Party. After that, I talked with Dr Shahrazad, who had great knowledge of history. Ali Sarmadi spent a lot of time with me and taught me numerous things theoretically and about history. Bahman Radmerikhi (Pil Aghazi) who was a carefree, happy, and strict, talked about the Organization of Iranian People's Fedai Guerrillas at some sessions. In room number four, there were some other people including Mansour Bazargan, Mr Sahabi, Mr Reza Malekmohammadi,

Nabi Moazami, and Habib Mokramdust, who were all members of the People's Mojahedin Organization of Iran, except Mr Sahabi, who was a member of the Nehzate Azadi (Freedom Movement Party). Moazami was a member of Mojahedin and had been shot in the leg in an armed confrontation. Room 17, Hamid Arz, Peiman Khandan were members of Organization of Iranian People's Fedai Guerrillas. Dr Fazlolah Hoshdaran, who was a member of SETAREIE SORKH (Red Star Party) and they were from the medical university of Shiraz; they spent time with me as well. I had some classes with Dr Karimi and Dr Ansari that helped me a lot. Mr Reza Bakery, who was a member of the Mojahedin Organisation, who had changed his ideology, was a popular man; his brother was a member of the Mojahedin Organisation and had been executed in 1350 (1971).

I met all of them in room 15. Mohammad Haghighat who was a member of ARMANE KHALGH organisation and had lots of memories of Homayoun Katiraei. Once, he told a story about a day when he had been called by an interrogator to go to a room where Homayoun was. "I saw that Homayoun was sitting on a seat, and apparently, he was not feeling okay and his skin colour had turned to red. After that day, once I asked him about the reason; he told me that they had put an electrical heater under his seat and the seat was hot as hell, but he was trying to smile not to let anyone know anything about the awful situation."

Seiied Jalil Seiied Ahmadi, was member of the Mojahedin Organisation, who had changed his ideology and gone through special training courses in ALFATH camp. He was such a gentleman. Homayoun Hajikhani was condemned with Khalil Paknia and Farzad Honarpishe for the same crime. He learned barbery services in the prison, and in his free time, he would cut the prisoners' hair.

He was such a hospitable and kind man. Naser Aghajari was from the Agha Jari neighbourhood and was also a school teacher. Saeid Poor Abdullah, Taghi Razi, Fani, Soleimani, Kamran Changizzade, who were all students, and had been arrested in Shiraz. Javad Karimi, who was brother of Dr Mehdi Karimi, and Masoud Ganjou, who were students had been arrested in Shiraz, and many other university students who would usually be kept in prison for a short time. Siavash Mirzade who was a poet, and Akbar Masoum Beigi who ised to call him wrestler guerrilla.

Hosein Ghazi, Dr Kazem Shadvar had physical problems always, as they had burnt his waist with iron; deep wounds that would sometimes bleed. He used to exercise alone and not let anybody see that he was bleeding.

Had become so tired. Faraj Sarkouhi, the man of book, tea, and cigarettes, was a real open- minded person. Mehdi Ghabraei was a member of SETARE SORKH and was into literature, and he helped me a lot about literature and poem.

Alireza Zomorodian, a quiet, smiley, into studying books, and it was realy hard to get in touch with him. Her sister, Leila Zomorodian, had been killed by SAVAK in an armed confrontation.

Aziz Ghafari, from Dezful and one of the members of SETARE SORKH, was one of the naughty boys of the cell. Rahim Kiavar, one of the members of guerrilla organistation, was always smiley. Abdullah Puzesh and Gholamhosein Puzesh, Reza Farmahini were considered as one of the old activists. Ali Dalil Safaei was always quiet, and I got the chance to talk with him several times. His brother, Seifollah Dalilsafaei, was one of the first members of guerrillas, and in 1350, had been executed. Mohammad Ali Rahmani one of the Mojahedin Organisation members was a real gentleman.

Abbas Davari, with a lovely Turkish accent, was always smiling and one of the members of the Mojahedin Organizationwho was a tailor; soon, he was sent to Tehran once again after fundamental changes in the Mojahedin Organisation interrogation. Sohrab Moeini used to always walk alongside Hamid ArzPeima; he was from Khusestan Province, so hospitable, but it was not so easy to get in touch with him.

Members of SAKA were mostly in touch with each other in their own group. Saeid Alizade, Hadi Pakzad, Dr Tabatabaei were all in one room. Once Saadi invited me to their room. Haj Tagha, Akbar Hadad, and Mr Taheri were religious and were familiar with social issues. I got to talk with them sometimes specially Akbar Hadad, who I met at some points after being released from prison. Fathollah Khamenei, one of the members of the Mojahedin Organisation who changed his ideology, smiley, active and due to 19th of Bahman, he had made a guerrillas logo with dough, and I was lucky to talk with him several times. Farzad Honarpishe, a quiet, mysterious man who used to wear eye glasses, and was so lovely and hospitable. Khalil Paknia who was a fellow citizen of Farzad, and they were condemned over a same crime case; he was an university student in English. Mr. Balghourian who was a member of Democratic Party of Iranian Kurdistan and had been in prison by then for 15 years; so many years in Borazjan prison, and after, that he was sent to Shiraz.

Majid Amin Moed, a skilful translator who I didn't get to talk with that much, 31th Farvardin 1354, that we got access to newspapers in the prison; no one could believe a piece of news that had been published about killing eight prisoners in Evin Prison who had been shot due to running away from the prison. Prisoners discussed a lot about the issue; that day, almost all prisoners came to exercise yard, and I was wondering what was going on.

31th Farvardin 1354, due to Sabeti's order and kings confirmation, they killed nine people including two members of the Mujahedin Organisation, Mostafa Khoshdel and Kazem Zolanbar and other members of the Fedai's Organisation. Bijan Jozei, Hasan Zarifi, Ahmad JalilAfshar, Aziz Sarmadi, Ahmad Choupanzade, and Souraki due to a fake charge of escaping from the prison. General Vaziri and some other interrogators of SAVAK had assassinated them.

This event, and its real story, was revealed by Tehrani, a famous interrogator of SAVAK, after the revolution.

After exercising, all prisoners started to discuss about the problem in some groups and every prisoner had a different attitude towards the event. We were warned not to do anything by the guards as they were totally prepared for confrontation. I walked alongside Parviz Ghaemian and Naser Mahani.

Javid Pashaei helped make a plan for studying and increase my knowledge and make the most of my time.

We were asked to go to court once again; this time, we met the lawyer and went through our case to get ready for the main court. In court, I also I got to meet my mom, who had come to the court to meet me, and we went back to the prison after that. I had a problem with writing my statement of defence; I consulted with some people on how to write a good one. Javid helped me a lot, and after some days, I completed it based on the Bushehr situation. In my statement of defence

I mostly explained about Bushehr's awful situation. I myself was from one of the poor neighbourhoods of Bushehr.

My mom was waiting for me outside of court.

I had a lot of stress in court day. Adibpour, deputy of the prison, rude and impolite, was from Ahvaz and was executed after the revolution by Khalkhali, came to us and asked us some questions as well, then we were sent to the court. We had to give our statement of defence to the prison's office to sign to be able to take it to the court. After reading it, he slapped my face. I was dizzy. He called it bullshit and started to shout at me and asked who has written it for me. I said I decided what to write, and he looked at me angrily, crumpled the paper, and threw it at me. As always, we went to the military court in a minibus.

When we got there, my mom was waiting for us in front of the court. She had been told to make me ask for forgiveness; they thought this way I could easily get released. My reaction to my mom's request was only a smile. Our lawyers asked us to show them our statement of defence. They got angry and asked why we didn't apologize to the king. And we all said we didn't want to be forgiven, and we wanna continue our life in the prison; soon afterwards, were guided to the main court session.

The courtroom was a large hall with five seats in front of us as defendants, with the presiding judge, Colonel Molaei, in the middle, and two other colonels sitting on either side of him.

The prosecutor sat to the right, in the middle under the tribune of the court clerk, and to the left were our lawyers. We went in and sat on the chairs dedicated for defendants. Behind us, there were several chairs where the policemen were sitting, and among them, there was a policeman who was from Bushehr who had a little fun with us before the trial. The clerk announced for us to stand. The presiding judge entered. Five other high rank military officers entered the court following him. They sat down and after introducing ourselves, the prosecutor started talking and pointing at us. The court atmosphere had impressed me in such a way that I did not understand what the prosecutor said, and then the lawyer talked a lot, and it was my turn to read my statement of defence.

I stood. I read my statement of defence, which was about the situation of poverty and misery and the problem of Bushehr villages and the bad economic situation of Bushehr, which was the reason for our protest against the Shah. I was frowned upon by the lawyer and the other guys read their defence and the trial ended, and we were said that we would be informed of the result at prison. When I was leaving the court, the same Bushehr policeman came to me and said I told the truth perfect. Finally, one of the people of Bushehr said something. Once again, I met my mom and we came back to my cell; and everyone started to ask us questions about the court and things that happened. I explained the entire day in detail to everyone. Some of the prisoners started to predict the result of the court as well. But I was happy that even if I had to stay in prison for a long time, I could make the most out of my time. Finally, they gave the verdict of guilty. One and a half years for me, and one year for each of my friends. So I knew that for the next one and a half years, I had to stay there, so I made a comprehensive plan for the upcoming days to make the most out of my time. Javid was a great help for me during that time.

I continued exercising in the afternoon. And I planned to talk about the freedom movement with Engineer Sahabi and the Tudeh Party, Kimanesh in relation to the Fada'is, which was my main issue. I had class with Hamid Arzepima, Mahmoud Mahmoudi, Ali Sarmadi, and Setareh Sorkh with Aziz and the Mojahedin with Abram Avakh, Fatah Ahl Khamenei, and Mr Reza Bakeri, especially Massoud Ismail Khani, I had a class. Mansour Bazargan enthusiastically explained about the Mojahedin. Mansour Bazargan was the brother of Pouran Bazargan and the wife of Fatemeh Amini and was the first Mujahideen woman to be tortured to death by SAVAK.

I talked to Bani Moazami about AL-FATH bases. Saadi Alizade explained SAKA to me. Once again, they announced that we had to go to the second instance court; I had to write another statement of defence, but I didn't write down anything and went to the court, and I said that my statement of defence is the one I gave to the court the last time. They didn't like my words, and it was not important for me at all. We went back to the prison. After some weeks, it was clear that based on the last and definite verdict of the appellate court, I was sentenced to jail for two years, and another friend of mine was sentence d to jail for one and a half years, and the other one for one year. I was in room number 15; there were three old officers there who had been in prison for 23 years, and I couldn't get along with them easily. So I had to get used to living there in its specific condition.

I was curious about the Tudeh Party, and before entering the prison, I was against them. I got know them more and more as I was living in the same room with them. Mr Keimanesh was such a gentleman and would speak to me sometimes and explain about the Tude Party and their role between 1320 (1942) and 1332 (1953).

He used to be in the military, and he explained how he used to give secret information to Tudeh members before being arrested. He meant that he would inform members in advance when they were about to get arrested so that they had more time to run and avoid arrest. Mr Amouei was the greatest member in the room about political issues; it was really hard to get in touch with those people because he was always busy and didn't have free time to talk.

Mr Keimanesh helped me to have some sessions with Mr Amouei, and I told them my father's story, which was interesting to them.

Mr Abbas Hejri, who was a quiet man and used to study a lot, during this time I was in room 15; I had no clear ideology. I would always try not to stay in room for long. I was so eager to be in touch with armed guys and learnhow to fight and in general how to fight in prison. Not to get tired in prison and be released after my jail sentence proudly. I had to learn how to get used to the prison's situation. I was young and so energetic and had a short prison sentence. I did my best to get in touch with all types of political groups and get more information about them. Mr Taheri also explained about 15th of 1342 (1963) events and their protests and also about Reza Dibaj, who had been murdered by Dehghan Bazju. I talked a lot with Ebrahim Avakh about Mujahedin. He also played an important role in making me think about my ideologies once again because he used to wrap up and categorise all issues for me.

I also used to talk a lot with Esmaeil Khani about different issues. I was into talking with him as he had changed his ideology. I also tried several times to get to talk with Taghi Afshani; he promised me, but unfortunately, he didn't give me a chance to talk. After that I got in touch with people from other groups, specially those who had changed their way after 1352 (1973) riot. I was also lucky to get the chance to talk with

Dr Ahmadi several times, who was one of the Fedai Guerrillas members and talked about some interesting items as well. He was responsible for medicine, and every day, he would come to the cell with his hand full of medicine and give them to those who needed them. I also got to talk with Dr Ahmad Zarkesh, who was one of the few survivors of SETAREIE SORKH (red star party). I was in prison for nine months until I started to deal with depression, and suddenly, I fainted in front of the toilet. Dr Ahmadi and Dr Houshdaran were worried about me, so they made a group, and they ordered some items from the outside of prison for me because of my physical weakness.

Mr Keimanesh put lots of his efforts into taking care of me and did his best to entertain me. We went to the exercise yard several times, and he explained many details about life in prison.

They arranged a class for me with Davoud Solhdoust, which was about economy and also let me listen to Mr Amoei when he was holding class in the room. He started to explain the history of the Tudeh Party, which was so important to me. I had just turned eighteen, so hormonal changes had caused me to become a little depressed. But soon afterwards, I got to control myself once again. But, honestly, I had problem with the Tudeh Party, so I couldn't stay with them.

One of the great things that members of the Tudeh Party used to care about was helping those prisoners who would get sick and tired of living in prison and at some point couldn't stand living in prison anymore; they wouldn't let them lose their hope, and I really think that was a great help for all prisoners.

I tried to change my room. After asking the guards, I was sent to room number three. Room three was totally different with room 15. Room 15 had a comprehensive plan for handling every thing, but room three was totally different and didn't have a clear plan at all, which was a clear sign that people in room 15 had a plan for living in prison.

In Room three, Ebad Ahmadzadeh was one of the first members of the the Tabriz branch of the guerrilla organization, known as the student of Samad Kazem and Behrooz, and I had heard a lot about him when I to the prison in the first place, but now I was in the room where he lived. He was tired and was just serving his sentence. But Mahmoudi, that I would never lose the chance to be in his classes, he used to consider himself as the only survivor of Siahkal and was Ghafor Hassanpour's sympathizer. In fact, he believed that we should learn to be feasible and independent. Room three was a preparation room for me to go out and join the fight, and it was a team house. And I completely lost touch with the Tudeh Party members.

STUDY AND RESEARCH IN PRISON

I attended some different classes. One day, new prisoners who had been just arrested in Bandar Abbas were brought to the cell. They were so noisy, and I became friends with some of them which, last even until after the revolution.

Rasoul Nikpour, who was a musician o utside of the prison, used to hold English classes as well because they would always say that outside the prison, some books of Marx-Lenin could be found.

After a while, Mahmoud went to the room in which Hamid Arzpeima used to also live, so room three was not interesting to me anymore. I tried to change my room until they took Saeid Ghazian to our room. He was sentenced to prison due to translating some booklets with Mr Batouei. Saeid was arrested, but Btouie, no! So it was clear to us that Batouie was the one who had exposed us in Bushehr!

Batouie was arrested in 1350 (1971) and had been released by promising SAVAK to cooperate, and after, he started to live in exile in Bushehr as a teacher. Batouie used to hold a Quran class during revolution and also managed a public library. After revolution, he was arrested for a short period of time, but he was released very soon. Saeid Ghazian was in prison for one year; during that time, we mostly spent our time together not as teacher and student, but as two political prisoners! Saeid explained that he was supporter of Hamid Tavakoli, a member of the guerrilla organization. He said when he was a university in student in Mashhad, he was arrested just due to this reason for a short time. Saeid said he used to work with Batouei on some projects, so without any doubt, he was the one who gave information to SAVAK about us as he had some information about me through him.

After one year, he was released. Following him, Khorshid Faghih, who had been arrested in Gachsaran-Aghajari, came to the cell. He was one of the best teachers of Bushehr. We would talk a lot. Eidi Nemati and his brother Eskandar were arrested in the same event. Nabi was sent

41

to Evin prison soon afterwards, and after the revolution, I met him at guerrilla headquarters. I was sent to room four.

Engineer Sahabi, Mansour Bazargan, Mr Reza Malek Mahmoudi, and Nabi Moazemi were in the room. Nabi Moazami was the one I really liked. He was one of the Mujahedin members and was killed in 1360.

Once I read a piece of news about the assassination of Bahram Aram in the newspaper, and after that, Ebrahim Avakh explained a lot about him and Mujahedin, which was one of my good memories from the prison.

Tir 8, 1355 (1976)!!! The cell was in absolute silence. As usual, we got the newspaper at two o'clock. The headline on the front page read that the leader of terrorists was killed. Hamid Ashraf was the leader of the Iranian People's Fedai Guerrillas Organisation. All prisoners went to the exercise yard, and they started to walk along side each other and talked about the issue. They were all so angry, and they couldn't believe that the legendary guerrilla Hamid was killed. Almost all prisoners took part in that day's exercise, and while doing exercise, they sang prison poems in a low voice. While they were walking in the yard, they would take an angry look at guards when they faced them, which would provoke the guards. The ward guards went into the guard room and locked the entrance to the ward. At dinner, only the workers were called to go to the guard just by mentioning their names and taking delivery of the dinner.

We could feel something was going to happen. Mahmoud gathered us in room three and said, "Be careful, the police are ready to create another repression like 1352 (1973) and be very aware." He gave a short talk on the history of Hamid Ashraf and his role in the guerrilla movement. With the silence and anthem of the Fadaei Khalq organization, he finished his words. I had memorised almost all anthems of the prison, and I would sing them in a low voice at any situation, and I was getting prepared to be released from prison. Because Bahman (Febreaury) was the month that I was supposed to be released, and I knew that I would not be released, I would have to go through a period of MELLIKESHI (something like nationalisation).

MELLIKESHI was the king's plan exactly like Israel prisons that they would keep prisoners for a longer time. Some prisoners were in touch with the organisation and could connect a trusted prisoner from inside the prison to the organisation. Due to this, SAVAK would try to keep prisoners for a longer time so that if they had fixed to do something afterwards, it would be automatically cancelled.

Anyway, there was no hope in getting released from prison. When my mom came to visit me and said I would stay in Shiraz until I was to be released, I said they are not going to release me, and their new strategy is not to release prisoners soon, and we had to do Mellikeshi. My mom burst into tears, and she she left the room while crying. She was there after coming from Busher which was seven hours from my place. This was the time when the the Liberation Organization of Iran's people was going through a hard time; the news was published in the newspaper that Parviz Vaezzadeh and his wife Masoumeh Tavafchian, Khosrow Safaei, Gsyuz Boroumand and Mahvash Jasemi were killed. Jasemi and Shokooh Tavafchian were killed while being tortured. Soon, some rumours started to go around that Sirus Nahavandi was behind the story who escaped in a fake escape by SAVAK and managed to organize this process. It was said that this news had been told by Saeid Soltanpour, who used to live abroad. In those years, numerous people were arrested in Iran. And the prison was becoming full of prisoners.

Most of the new prisoners were members of the Liberation Organization. I was also preparing to be released. Some rooms used to invite me to join them. And I went to most of the rooms. Just the room of religious people didn't invite me. It was when those religious prisoners had decided not to be in touch with people from other groups. I went to Mr Keimanesh's room, and that was my last meeting with him. Back then, Mahmud had already been sent to Ahvaz. But before being sent to there, he had asked me to give his message to Hosein Khoshnevis, who used to be in ward one and had told me lots of good things about him. I tried to make a connection in a way with the organization, but I couldn't make it happen. I had heard that I needed to go to Palestine (they meant people's front party for the liberation of Palestine, which was led by George Habash), and some people would say go to Tehran; over there they can fine released prisoners and a make a connection. I had decided to do my best to make a connection with the organisation because it had become so difficult to make a connection with the organisation members after 1355 (1976) event. So, I made my decision to go to Palestine camp or abroad at all costs. Other prisoners used to give example of Esmaeil Abedini, who had been able to a make connection with the organisation after 1355 (1976), and he was killed by SAVAK.

GETTING RELEASED FROM ONE PRISON AND BEING SENT TO ANOTHER

It was time for freedom. I packed all my stuff, and I waited with the same black slippers of the prisoners until the guard came to open the door. Kamoun gave me some money to have in my pocket when I go out. One week before freedom, I was asked to go to the administrative section of the prison. A fashionable man in a tie was sitting at the table and shook my hand and told me to sit down. I sat. He asked my name and after writing the details. He gave me a piece of paper to sign that included a commitment to make sure I wouldn't participate political activities anymore, and if anyone came to me for this purpose, I would inform SAVAK. I said I wouldn't sign. After threatening and insulting, he said that if I don't sign the paper, I wouldn't be released. He called the guard led me to the ward. When I explained to other prisoners, they said the man I had met was a well-known member of SAVAK called Dehghan, and he had also killed Mohammadreza Dibaj. I got out of the ward. The corridor of the prison that I had looked at scarily, now I was looking at it with regret as I was not going to meet the people in the prison again in my life.

The prison gave me the opportunity to learn about human relationships. Anyway, I went with the guard, and they said I was free and asked if I had anything in the warehouse. I said yes, and we went to the prison warehouse behind the kitchen, and I had some stuff there. They gave them to me, and we went to the guard's officer room. I signed the prison paper and waited to get out. But the guard officer told me to go to another room to wait. After a while, they called me and said "Let's go".

I asked where.

They said I would understand in the future. Once again, I was handcuffed. I said "I'm free".

They said I was only being freed from that prison. We left the prison with two guards by Peikan car. I didn't know anywhere in Shiraz; we were going to an unknown place. We were on the road for a long time until we stopped in front of a big door. The door opened, and we went in.

It was the Shiraz Joint Anti-Sabotage Committee. They were the committee guards who took me over. The SAVAK committee was on Shahpour Street, behind Karim Khan Citadel, in front of Bank Melli, and the Shiraz Agahi Wall. Anyway, they took me to an office. From that moment, the sound of screaming and shouting could be heard. I was shocked and scared. We entered the office. Two young men were being interrogated. I stood in the corner of the room. A man in a tie came and asked my name and asked very slowly if I came from ward four? I said yes! He pointed to the policeman to take me down for now.

I went down a few steps to the basement where someone was standing, and a blanket was thrown over his head. As soon as we arrived, the policeman hit the man on the head and said, "Are you taking a nap?"

It was clear that, according to the interrogator's order, he should stand and not sleep. We went to several rooms, all of which were full of prisoners, all handcuffed. To imagine it, there were some cells doors along the staircase as we were going down.

He said to go there until he found a place for me. I went and stood at a corner.

The sound of torturing and insults by the interrogators had made the atmosphere terrifying. I stood there for some hours, then the guard came once again, and he asked my name and my crime! I said I have come from ward four. Suddenly, he shouted and asked why I didn't say it earlier; he grabbed my hand, and we went upstairs. Once again, we went to the room the interrogator was in, and two people were being interrogated. The same man that I had met him in the prison one week ago, Dehghan, was in the room. Back in the prison, he was so gentle and would talk in a calm friendly way, but here the story was totally different. Here he would interrogate in a violent way by shouting, torturing, and insulting. He looked at me and said, "Do you come from ward four?" I said yes! He shouted at the guard and said "Why did you bring him here? Take him back to the down floor."

The guard replied that all the rooms were full, and there was no place for me.

He said take him to the corridor.

The guard took my hand and led me to the end of the corridor. It had a door that connected to the intelligence office. I stood there, and he said I was not allowed to sit. I said I was released from prison and why are you keeping me? The guard said he would ask the authorities, and maybe he could bring you a chair. A few hours passed, and the guard came with a chair.

He told me sit until I was called. The cries, screams , and curses of the interrogators filled the air. Anyway, it was time for lunch, and the guard brought me a plate of Adas polo (a typical Iranian food). He asked if I needed anything. I said I had to go to the toilet. They were not hard on me because I was not under interrogation. After having lunch, they called me, and I went to the same room; a man was sitting at the table that later I learned was Arman.

I sat in front of him, and he told me to tell him, and I asked what I was supposed to tell. He said about ward four and what was going on over there! I was informed before this day that I might be asked these kinds of questions, so I was ready. Prisoners in ward four told me that I should be careful about what I say because SAVAK is looking to find a connection between Kamoun and the prisoners. I said I used to live alone, and I was waiting to be released. Arman stood and slapped me across my face and said I should write down all the information about ward four. I said I had no information.

Arman said he knew everything about inside the prison and also got so many reports about you from inside the prison. I was young and inexperienced, so I answered if you have got information, okay, so why do you ask me these questions? Arman once again slapped me in the face. He said if I thought I was going to be released, I was completely wrong. I would be under their control, and I should tell them everything about the ward. I said as I used to live alone. I can only tell about my life in the prison. He said to answer every question in detail. Suddenly, someone slapped me on the neck from behind. When I turned, I saw it was Dehghan.

One of the people in the room who was being interrogated looked at me, and he was wondering why I wasn't being tortured. I said out loud that I have already passed my prison sentence. "Why don't you release me?" I wanted to tell those two people that were being interrogated that I had come from prison to there.

They were university students from Shiraz who were arrested in connection with the Liberation Organisation. One had been severely tortured, and he couldn't easily walk. He was brought to the room to be interrogated. He looked at me angrily when he saw me sitting on the chair without being tortured, Dehghan approached him and slapped him few times.

They started to interrogate him. Arman and Dehghan went to him, and they left me alone.

A guard came, took my head, and took me to the downstairs. While going there, I saw some cells full of prisoners. He took me to the corridor again, which was connected to intelligence office. I said I had to go to the toilet. He waited for me behind the door. After getting back to the end of the corridor, I saw there was no chair there anymore. He said I could sit on the floor. While I was sitting, I unconsciously fell asleep until a guard beat me and said don't sleep. Once again, I explained that I was coming from ward four, and they had given me a chair here.

He asked where I was from. I said Bushehr. He replied, "I'm from Borazjan too," and after talking for some seconds, he turned out to be a distance relative of our family. He said he would l bring a chair and said to tell him whatever I needed. I said I was thirsty. He brought a chair and water for me, and I sipped a little water as I was also afraid of them not letting me go to the toilet after drinking too much. I took a nap there; they called me, and I went to the interrogation room. I saw Dehghan, who was next to that guy. He looked at me and went to the university students; I sat on a chair. Arman talked to me and told the guard to take me back.

I was again taken to the corridor, and they brought dinner for me. I ate and asked the guard to let me go to the toilet and brush my teeth, and he let me. From the other side of the wall, I could hear people shouting and crying. I was under a lot of pressure. A guard gave me a mattress, two blankets, and a pillow. I couldn't sleep a wink till morning. Dehghan had come back to the building after drinking too much, and he continued beating people, insulting them, interrogating in the middle of the night. I could hear moaning. The following day, I went to Arman in the afternoon once again.

He said this is your re-arrest paper that you need to sign. After that, I was taken to the first place once again. I could see guards going up and down stairs to take people to be tortured and interrogated. Last time that I met Arman, he told me if I wanted to get free, I needed to tell him all I knew about ward four, and again, I came up with a same answer. I was looking outside through a window in his room. He said he knew I missed being free, but they would never let people like me live outside again as I start to kill people. After three days, I was sent to Adel Abad prison once again; on the way to the prison, there were those two university students in the car. One of them looked at me angrily; I figured out he was suspicious of me as I was not tortured, so I decided to explain my story to them until we got there, but that after saying few words, the guard stopped me from talking.

The guard officer said again, "You? I thought you were going to be released"? We were sent to ward one. Those two were taken to the second floor, and I was guided to the first floor. Hosein Khoshnevis was also there, and I gave him Mahmoud Mahmoudi's message. The prison had become full of new prisoners from the Liberation Organisation. Hosein Khoshnevis was a skinny friendly man, who had a problem in his right wrist as he had tried to commit suicide once when he was being tortured by SAVAK. So, I decided to spend my prison sentence in ward one based on the experiences that I had gained from ward four. Some university students had been arrested in connection to 16th of Azar, and most of them would be released from ward one. One of my duties was to collect articles from Keihan newspaper. Amir Taheri or Mesbah Zade would choose and write them, and we would discuss them with each other.

Once, when I was walking in the yard, a university student came to me and asked to walk alongside me. He asked some questions about ward four. He regretted that he had not found the chance to meet a beautiful girl, and that he had tried to blow her mind as he had been arrested.

There was a German prisoner, Peter. He had been arrested due to drug dealing. We tried to get in touch with him to get more information about Baader-Meinhof, but it seemed like he didn't know him. There was also this guy, Hamid Dehbozorgi, in ward one that had hit several students in Shiraz with his car, who had insulted SANDAL SIAH (she was a famous owner of a brothel in Shiraz); however, he had to be executed according to his crime, but SANDAL SIAH had great connections with top authorities, so they didn't execute him. He wouldn't eat prison's food at all, and he would respect us as well. Once he also ordered food for Hosein and he didn't accept it and said he had already gotten used to prison food. Hosein was arrested around 197 , he was in the same team with Kazem, Javad Salehi, and Ebrahim Afsorde.

In ward one, many members of the Liberation Organisation were kept, and no one could believe that Nahvandi had cooperated with SAVAK, and the had been organised by them. Hosein had asked me to always keep some food, clothing , and medicine secretly in our cell for those who were brought to the prison after tough interrogations.

Once a week, we would gather in a room. We would read some poems and anthems that we had learned while serving our prison sentence in ward four, and we would also teach them to new prisoners. When a guy whose name was Naser Mahani entered the prison, we started to exercise much more professionally. There were some religious guys who were not eager to take part in our activities. We were surprised when we got a piece of news from ward four that some members of the SEPASI Party had been released in Tehran. I had hidden some articles of Keihan newspaper under my mattress, which had become a great archive by then.

SHAH, CARTER, AMNESTY INTERNATIONAL, AND HUMAN RIGHTS

S epas celebration (a special celebration back in Pahlavi dynasty) was held in February of 1979. Mohammad Reza Pahlavi released some political prisoners due to Carter's policies about Human rights that was broadcast on TV and became well-known as Sepas. To name some of the most famous prisoners that were released back then, Asgar Olaei and Karoubi should be mentioned. Once in the evening, Khalghi came and said, "I want to conduct a cell search". We had experienced these types of cell searches in ward four but in ward one, it was happening for almost the first time. Back in ward four, they would conduct a cell search every four or five weeks, and it had become routine. But in ward one, as we didn't have any connection with the outside of the prison, conducting a cell search seemed to be a little bit unusual. I didn't let Khalghi enter my cell. Khalghi went to the guard office; meanwhile, I quickly took my article archive out of my cell.

Khalghi came back with two guards. I was standing in front of my cell. He pushed me aside angrily and started to inspect my cell. Hosein came and said, "What's going on here"?

Khalghi was going through the cell angrily to find something that seemed to be exposed; he didn't answer Hosein but found some medicine, clothing, and food that I used to keep in my cell. He took them out of the cell. Kamran, a Melli Kesh from Shiraz, came and didn't let him take stuff out of the cell. Khalghi and Kamran had a little argument. Khalghi angrily pushed me and Kamran aside and went to the office guard. Hosein told others not to gather in front of the cell, and he said we should wait for the consequences. These things all happened in days that prison authorities had been ordered not to put too much pressure on political prisoners as Amnesty International was going to come to the prison and check the situation closely, so they had also repaired broken glasses left from 1974 riot in the prison, in addition to providing some better facilities for the prisoners.

Anyway, after a while, Khalghi came back alongside three other guards. They came straight to me and wanted to take me with them.

Khalghi was also angry with Kamran because of their argument, so they took both of us. It was around 7 p.m.; the guard officer and some guards were waiting for us outside the ward. Khalghi started to explain about things that happened earlier and said that Kamran and I had intended to beat them. As Kamran wanted to talk, they slapped him in the face. I shouted at them to support Kamran, and he slapped me on the face as well. He started to insult us and sent us to solitary confinement, and said he would decide what to do about us tomorrow.

Those solitary confinements were located behind the kitchen, next to the cold store of the prison, which was so hot during summers and so cold during winters. These cells were also used to keep prisoners who were going to be executed, 48 hours before their execution. It was also used to punish prisoners who were not following the rules. In those rooms, prisoners had to be kept naked just with underpants, and there was also a torn blanket over them. Anyway, they took us there that night, which was so cold as we were in the last month of winter. We could smell sweat, blood, and all dirty things, and two dirty blankets. Fortunately, there were no louse in those blankets. First, our bodies were warm, but after a while, we started shivering from winter's cold. Kamran suggested exercising to get warm, but exercising didn't work. We wrapped ourselves in the blanket. The floor was cold. If we had laid them on the floor, we wouldn't have had any blanket left to cover ourselves with; we did our best to keep ourselves warm by exercising till morning; that was the only possible way. They had also told us that we were not allowed to go to the toilet till morning, which was also a problem itself.

The following day in the morning a guard came and gave us tea, a piece of bread, and cheese.

After having breakfast, the room again became cold. Kamran suggested going on a hunger strike. Kamran asked the guard in front of the room to bring us a pen and a piece of paper. He opened the door angrily and asked what we wanted. Kamran said we were going on a hunger strike, and we wanted pen and paper to write down our situation. Those days they were so cautious of their behaviour towards prisoners as Amnesty International was supposed to inspect the prison in upcoming days. After two or three hours, they brought us lunch; we refused it and said we have already started our hunger strike, and once again, we asked for a pen and a paper. After a while, he came back with a pen and paper. Kamron wrote down that as the officer guard insulted us without any reason or giving us any opportunity to explain, he should come to us and apologise; otherwise, we would continue our hunger strike, and we wouldn't go to the visiting room to visit those who would come to visit us. We both signed the paper and gave it to the guard.

According to what we had heard several times about others who had gone on strike, we decided to thoroughly control the quality and the time that we were going to spend on exercising, walking, and other activities carefully so we didn't lose our energy. We only asked the guard to give us either tea or boiled water with sugar because we had gone on a wet strike. (there are two kinds of strike in prison, Wet and Dry, in the Wet strike tear or water with sugar could be drunk but in Dry strike a person wouldn't eat or drink anything.) After a while, I went to the toilet, and I came across Ghasem Jafari, who was one of the roughneck prisoners in the ward. I had previously met him in ward one, and he knew that I had been kept in ward four during my prison sentence. He had heard about us being on a strike. This guy was executed later in the famous 1980 riot, which happened in Rasht.

They knew that Kamran and I were on a strike. He said, "Do you need anything"? I said only some fags of cigarette and more tea and sugar. He could do that for us as these types of prisoners had good connection with the guards and I also asked him to inform prisoners in ward four that we were on a strike and kept in solitary confinement.

Prisoners in ward four didn't show a serious reaction, maybe because those days prisoners in ward four were calm, and our strike might have seemed a little bit more than enough for them. Anyway, they brought lunch and we said only tea; they brought us tea and sugar cubes from the room behind us. Two plastic cups and sugar cubes that the guard said were items sent from Ghasem Jafari. We asked him to thank Ghasem

Jafari, and we asked the guard to give us extra blankets, but he said no. We didn't know whether we had to exercise because on the one hand, it was clear for how long we were going to stay on strike, on the other hand, it was so hard to stand those cold days and nights.

The guard brought dinner for us, and once again, we said we only want tea. As a result of drinking tea and boiled water, we needed to go to the toilet more often, which was against the room rule (in those rooms, prisoners were allowed to go to the toilet only three times a day), but it was clear that the guards were told to take it easy on us.

At ten o'clock, they brought some blankets for us that could keep us a little bit warmer. The following day, they brought us breakfast, but once again, we refused to eat, and we asked to meet one of the prison's authorities. A sergeant came and asked what we were going to do and what we had decided for the future. We said that the officer should apologize both of us. The sergeant smiled and left there sarcastically. That day, nothing special happened. The day after that, the officer whose name was Noushiravanpoor, a young well-mannered man, came and asked what our problem was. Kamran explained and said that they treated us roughly. He said in my opinion, go back to the ward and I will talk with head of the prison(head of the prison had changed and I can't actually remember his name now).

Kamran said, "What about apologizing"? He said we wanted something impossible; even if we die because of the strike, nothing will happen; so think wisely, and go back to the ward. After that, he left. We didn't eat lunch and dinner. The news about our strike had spread like a virus all around the prison by Ghasem Jafari. Fortunately, he was by our side. I only smoked half a cigarette as the cell was so small, and it would make it hard to breathe if we smoked more. Kamran generally wouldn't smoke at all, so I quitted smoking for a while. We also spent that night with a physical weakness.

Ealy in the morning, another officer came and began to speak authoritatively about the powerful imperial state of Iran and said finish this strike yourselves, otherwise, we will put an end to your strike ourselves; then he left. We just listened to him without saying a word. While saying these things, he was standing outside the cell as he couldn't stand the smell. As the door had been kept opened for a while when he was talking, we got to breathe some fresh air. As we were on strike, guards would open the vision panel more often to make sure that fresh air would come in every now and then. The unpleasant smell would also annoy us. After not accepting lunch again, an officer came to us who was trying to act like a kind officer and said we were so young and should care more about our health.

Kamran said we had been on strike for five days, and so far, and the authorities haven't cared about our situation, unfortunately. This officer again asked us about our demands. And once again, we emphasised that the officer had to apologize. Around 9 p.m., the deputy of the prison came and said in a friendly way that tomorrow the officer would come, and it was better for us to go back to the ward. We consulted with each other, and we came to the conclusion that even if the deputy was lying, making the deputy come here to this room was a kind of victory. Around 10 p.m., a guard came to us and asked for our decision, and we said we would go back to the ward!

The guard brought us our clothes, and we went to ward one. As it was after lights-out, the guard said go into our cell quietly! Hosein realised that we were there; guards always behaved respectfully towards him, so they opened his cell door and said for now do not eat anything until he prepared some warm soup. We ended our strike. That officer never came to ask us for an apology, and we didn't ask anymore.

In the middle of Farvardin (first month of the Solar Hijri calendar, first month of spring season, April), they took most members of the Liberation Organisation to ward four. There were some religious prisoners and some other prisoners who were sentenced due to minor crimes besides us left in ward one. Religious prisoners wouldn't get in touch with us at all. One of the famous prisoners among them was Haj Tagha, who became Shiraz governor after the revolution, and Engineer Taheri, who became Kazerun (a city in south of Iran) district's member of parliament after the revolution for decades, and they had gathered few religious prisoners around themselves as well. Farvardin 1356 (April9, 1977) Keshvari, one of the prison guards we had chosen a nickname, Reza Khan, asked me to go to the guard's office. I went there, and as soon as I entered, he gave me the phone and told me to talk. It was the prison deputy who would always consider himself a democratic person;

he only had a good relations with Engineer Behpour, who had played an important role in helping him to graduate from university. That's why he would always try to show himself as a democratic person. Of course, during this time, Behpour also asked for amnesty and was released. Engineer Behpour was one of the first people who had connected the Mojahedin Organisation to the Al-Fath Organisation. Anyway, he asked my name and surname on the phone and added that if I wanted to be released, there was a paper that I needed to sign, and make a commitment to get released. I asked if it was what was keeping me in prison. I refused to sign and said I would stay in prison. He ended the call, and again, I went back to the cell. I talked with Hosein about what happened. The following day, they asked me to go to the office with my stuff. I packed my things and said goodbye to Hosein, and I left there. I didn't know to where I would be taken, but for sure, it was not to freedom.

I went to the guard's office. The guard, Khali, was there. He looked at me with embarrassment in a way to show me he was regretful for what he had done earlier. I asked what was going on. Why was asked to come there. He smiled and said they have decided to send me to ward four again. I was really happy, and I asked him to let me inform Hosein as well.

He allowed me to do so. I told Hosein about it and asked him if he had any message for prisoners in ward four. He said to just say hi on his behalf to the prisoners there.

I went to ward four, room five, where Professor Khatourian was kept. Soon afterwards, he made me understand not to get in touch with strangers, and he also told me try to live peaceably. In the beginning of May, which equals to 11th of Ordibehesht in the Persian calendar(second month of spring), we held a small secret celebration with the professor in the room and on that occasion, I got to know Rahim Banaei, who was a member of the Liberation Organisation that had been transferred to Shiraz recently. Once again, they asked me to go to the guard's office, and from there, I was taken to a luxury room. Dehghan had come to the prison to talk with me. He again repeated the same words that I would be free if I sign the paper and make a commitment not to continue political activities after prison and also if a person came to me, I had to inform SAVAK about the whole thing. I said I would make commitment not to continue political activities and if a person came to me, I wouldn't cooperate with them. I said I would only sign what I said, and I signed my words. I went back to ward four.

16th of Ordibehesht(May), the guard Rasti called and told me to pack my things and go to the guard's office. Once again, I said goodbye to the other prisoners, and I went to the office. Again, I was taken to ward one with another guard. I met Hosein again, and after greeting Khalghi, he took me to my room and locked it. Hosein was angry and spoke up for me, but they didn't care. I spent the entire day in that locked room. In the ward one, there were some university students who had been arrested recently and also in second and third floor there were some other prisoners who were there due to minor crimes . Allah Gholi Jahangiri organised a ward wide strike among ordinary prisoners. Allah Gholi was a political prisoner who had been transferred from Isfahan to Shiraz, but he was sent to the ward that was for ordinary prisoners as he was a son of a nobleman who was a well-known man, and Allah Gholi himself was so popular and beloved by others in his hometown. Allah Gholi went on a strike to protest against the prison's bad situation, guards' bad behaviour towards ordinary prisoners, and asking for some extra facilities in support of ordinary prisoners who had been taken to the second and third floor after a brutal beating. I got to know him there and I talked with him; he was so friendly, hospitable, and firm.

16th of Ordibehesht(May), once again, I was asked to go to the office. The guard, a young handsome man, was waiting for me in the office. After greeting and treating me in a respectful way, he said most prisoners who have signed the paper had been released. "Why are you still in prison? What's the matter"?

I said I signed it too. He said there were some points that needed to be corrected. I said in my opinion there is no point in it to be corrected. He smiled and asked me about my future plans after freedom. I said I have been in prison for two and a half years. He wished me good luck after freedom, shook hands, and left. I went back to ward one, and I talked with Hosein about it. He said most probably you will be freed from jail in the upcoming days. During this time, we would always try to help those ordinary prisoners who had been beaten in the prison. Allah Gholi was always optimistic and smiley.

19th Ordibehesht 1356(May9, 1977), they asked me to go to the office once again; it was around 11 a.m. The man from SAVAK was again there; he said I would be free if I changed some parts of my paper. I said I wouldn't change anything. He shook hands, and I went back to ward one. They brought lunch, and after having lunch, I got ready to make tea after receiving boiled water. A guard came and said happily I was free and to pack my things. He said he saw my freedom paper. Quickly, I went to Hosein and said goodbye to him and some other prisoners, and I packed my things in a plastic bag. It was sharp two in the afternoon, 19th of Ordibehesht, 1356 (May9, 1977). Yes, it was my freedom paper.

I signed the freedom paper, and I went to the guard's office, and there again I signed another paper. I was put in a Peikan car without handcuffs and blindfolds. We went to SAVAK on Zand Street. Over there, in a luxury room, a handsome man came and shook hands and said I was free. He asked how long I had been in prison? I said two and half years. He said no just two years. Those six months are not acceptable. I said I spent six months of my life in solitary confinement illegally without deserving it.

He talked for a while and said our country is on the way of progress and improving economically, and they needed people like me to improve the country for better, and he said I was free but should come back there tomorrow. I said I had no ID card, and I know nowhere in Shiraz to stay at night. He gave me the address of a lodging house on Zand Street named Chahar Fasl (it means four seasons) and said I have been sent from SAVAK, and they won't ask for any ID card. But I had to pay on my own. Kamoun had given me some money when I was getting free. I said I have money. I came out of SAVAK with the black slippers on and the plastic bag and another bag I had brought with when I was being transferred from Bushehr to Shiraz on the first day. I went to that address. I knew Shiraz a little bit, specially Zand and Darioush Streets!

I found the address, and I asked the receptionist for a room. He took a look at me and my appearance. I also had a small paper from SAVAK, which I showed him, and they gave me a room. Quickly, I put my stuff in the room and went down the street to eat a special Soltani kebab (a special delicious Iranian food), but on the way, my mind was busy with other prisoners' situations about what they were doing and some other stuff like what would happen after going back to Bushehr. I ate dinner while still my mind was busy, soon afterwards, I went back and slept as I had to go to SAVAK at eight o'clock in the morning. I woke early. I paid the cost, and I went to a restaurant to have breakfast. Afterwards, I went to SAVAK. And also, I had prepared myself if they were going to ask for anything that was against my want; I would go back to prison. The guard in the front office guided me to a room. I saw that some other university students who had been released during recent times were also over there. I said hello until a SAVAK officer came with a photographer.

I aasked why the photographer was here. The officer said the photo will be only kept here in their office.

While the photographer was taking pictures, I hid behind one of the university students so I wouldn't be in the picture. After taking pictures, he we could go, but he asked me to stay.

And again, they kept me in the room. After one hour, another officer came and said I should go back to Bushehr as soon as possible and inform SAVAK in Bushehr that I was back.

They asked when I was to go to Bushehr. I said I would go to Airport Boulevard and get a ticket. I came out of the SAVAK. With that black prison slipper on, I went to the Airport Boulevard, which was a passenger terminal. Back when I was brought to Shiraz for the first time, it took around seven hours to get there, so I thought to myself if get a ticket at 2 p.m., I will get to Bushehr at 9 p.m., and nobody would see me with that look. So I bought a ticket for 2 p.m. When I was walking around, I saw an acquaintance; he hugged and kissed me on the cheek, and he was so happy that I was released. I said I had to get a ticket to Bushehr for 2 p.m. I got on the bus at 2 p.m., and I went to Bushehr. The way between these two cities had changed a lot during these two and half years, and they had made lots of tunnels, which meant I would get to Bushehr earlier. It only took four hours. It was daylight when I got there. I took a taxi, the driver said, "Naser! Is that you"? He was one of my classmates back in high school who had become a taxi driver, and we were happy to see each other. We went to Sangi neighbourhood, and he stopped the taxi right in front of the Borazjanis mosque. He didn't get any money and said I was their pride and they were proud of me! I got out of his car. One of the guys in our neighbourhood who got to know me was standing in front of the mosque, shouting "Naser came back!" People came to me.

That was why I was hoping to get there at night because I didn't want to meet people that way. I was greeted warmly by the locals. We went towards our home while around 30 or 40 people accompanied me.

One guy entered the house and told my mom, "Nane Naser (it means mother of Naser)Naser came!" My mom couldn't believe it. I went into the yard, and as soon as my mom saw me, she fell to the ground half unconscious. After almost one hour, our yard was full of people. During my prison sentence, I had gotten used to having dinner at 7 p.m. I told my mom I needed to eat dinner. Quickly, they brought dinner for me, and all people around were wondering why I was having my dinner so early. They were all curious. They wanted to know about prison. Until 1 a.m., our home was filled of people. Some had brought some gifts. All my relatives were aware I had been released. During the next seven days, most all people came to meet me, and I was tired as based on life in the prison I would always wake at 7a.m., nd I had dinner at 7 p.m. My mind was always occupied by other prisoners' situation. The day after being freed, I had to go to SAVAK. I went there early in the morning. I met Iravani, and he said hoped I'd changed my previous bad habits and started life again, and even if I wanted to continue my studies in university, they would help with that. And then he gave me a paper and asked me to make a commitment that if a person came to me, I would inform them. I laughed and said I was in prison for six months more just because of this paper! And now he was asking me to sign it? "No, I won't sign it".

He started to shout at me and said he would send me back to prison. I said I had just come out, and I would stay here! He said I had thick skin! "You all enter prison as silly kid and when you come out you become a guerrilla".

He left the room and said, "Stay here!" Deep inside, I made myself ready to go back to prison once again.

It was noon. I was thinking to myself that somebody would come but no one came, so I started to walk in the room like walking in the cell, and I was thinking that what would happen. They didn't give me lunch. After an hour, a man I had never met him came in and said, "Let's go upstairs". We went where they had taken a picture of me on the first day, and again, they took a picture; it seemed like they were filing a new lawsuit. I told that SAVAK officer that I had not had lunch. He laughed and said it was normal. Again, I went back to the previous room, and after a while, Iravani came and asked if I had thought wisely. I said, "Mr. Iravani, what should I think about"? He answered that I should think about what he told you that if someone came to inform them. I said it seemed as if I should prepare myself for another six extra month in prison!

As he was leaving, I said I had not had lunch yet. He laughed and said, "We won't even give you a shit; it was five in the afternoon".

I heard a woman shouting at Iravani; it was my mom. She was asking why they were keeping me again. It was when I figured out that my sister and some of her friends had been arrested during mass arrest of 1355(1976), and they had been kept in SAVAK for a short time, and after that, they had been released. Finally, Iravani told my mom to go back to her home, and I would be released. My mom said she had been told that before, and she would stay this time until I was released.

Iravani said my mom was stubborn and to tell her to leave and go back home; he said to tell her I would be released and not to worry. I said she wouldn't believe me because she doesn't trust you! I told my mom, but she went and sat next to the sea, close to SAVAK.

Iravani came with another man, and they started to talk with me, and I said if anyone comes, I won't let you know about it. But I won't cooperate with him either. I have said before, I spent six more months for not signing the paper. Those days were exactly a time when Amnesty International Organisation members were in Iran and they were inspecting the prisons, so SAVAK had changed the way, they would treat people and they would try to treat all in a calm manner. At that time, I understood that they were in a position of weakness. Once again, they took my picture, and I went to the second floor and, came back to the first floor to the same room.

Around 5 or 6 p.m., Iravani came to the room once again and asked frowningly what I did last.

I said I wouldn't cooperate with anybody who comes to me, but I wouldn't inform SAVAK either. He said okay, I could go. He opened the door, and I left. I went to my mom, who was at the beach and said it's finished; let's go home.

We took a taxi home. All the people had been worried, so when we opened the door, we saw that our home was full of people, and my aunt poured a handful of candies on my head as she was happy, and we went and sat in the room. People were waiting for me to explain all things about those two and half years and also that day, but I just said I was tired, and they didn't continue.

GOING TO MILITARY SERVICE
OR PALESTINE

A fter one or two weeks, I started to look for a job. I was thinking either to go into military service or to Palestine. But military service was the best choice because I could become soldier within two years, and I would learn how to use a weapon, and I could find a better job as soon as I returned.

Gendarmerie would take those who had served one and half years in prison directly into the military, but I was in prison for two and half years, so I didn't know what their decision would be. One day, I went to gendarmerie with my ID card to announce I was ready to start my military service. My uncle was the deputy. I went to his office and said I was there to go into the military service.

One of them sitting at the table took a look at me and said with a laugh, "Isn't he your sister's son"? Everyone laughed; another one said he wanted to go into the military service, and they all laughed.

My uncle sat; he was a little bit angry due to his colleagues behaviour and told me in a kind way they wouldn't let me in. He asked why I wanted to join.

I said if I can go into the military, according to the law, I wanted to go. My uncle told me to think of my mother and all she had been through because of me. A man told my uncle I could be exempted from military service and asked how many years I was in prison.

I told him, and he said I didn't need to go to military service according to the law. I said okay, but what if still I want to go? He said I couldn't. Bring 6 photos so I can issue a deprivation card for you. You are deprived from all social rights.

I went home. I had not told my mom that I had decided to go into the military service. In front of our home was a big square where children would usually play football. I saw a man standing on the other side of the square with a bicycle!!!

I realised he was a stranger. I asked my mom how he had been standing there? She looked at him and said she didn't know and didn't know him!

I said I thought he was one of SAVAK members and we needed to be careful and see how long he would stay. I pretended I wanted to buy cigarette s so I went to a grocery store on the other side of our alley and his owner was named Iraj. I stood in front of his store and started to talk with Iraj.

The cyclist passed by us and took a look at us; it was when I was sure he was a SAVAK member.

According to what I had heard back in prison, it was how SAVAK would control some released political prisoners. I went back and told my mom I saw him, and he left. I told my mom if he came again, please check the time and also when he leaves. I got dressed and went to the street.

I talked with a driving instructor named Khodakhast and said I wanted to learn to drive and asked the cost. He said it was free for me. We fixed a time to start the classes. I notice a person following us. I told Khodakhast not to be afraid! But I guess SAVAKI members are following us! He said, "Are you kidding me"? I said no.

I asked about the time that we had already fixed for learning. He said we'd set another time in the future. We pulled over and the instructor got behind the wheel, and we drove outside the city. SAVAKI members were still after us. We went around Sabz Abad and Bahmani, which was one hour from Bushehr and then we came back. They were still following us.

It was kind of fun to Khodakhast, but for me, questioned why they were following me everywhere. He took me home and left. This man followed me for days, and it had become a kind of fun thing and also a question.

I stayed home for some days, and my mom would also buy me cigarettes whenever she would go out to buy things for home. That's when my mom alerted me that the cyclist had come around again.

My mom went to our neighbour's house. Our neighbour had three or four adult girls in their home, and they were so protective of those girls. They were Turk immigrants of Shiraz who moved to Bushehr and would live in the Sangi neighbourhood.

My mom told our neighbour that she thought the cyclist was skirt-chasing; they went once or twice outside and looked at that man and again they went in.

The father of the family was named Khodarahm, who had a gharry and used to work with it. His wife went to the cyclist and asked what he wanted and why he was standing there. They quarrelled, and other neighbours came to the square. She shouted that this man has come to womanize!

I was watching the scene through a small window in the house facing the square. Women in our neighbourhood surrounded him, and he fled. One of the women said to get the gendarmerie and bring a police officer and not let the man come into our neighbourhood again. That was the last day he came to the square.

One day, I went to the education department of our city and requested to continue my studies. A person whose name was Mirshekari and in reality was the agent of SAVAK in the education department saw my request and said he recommend I find a new job, and I wouldn't be accepted to continue my education. I was disappointed.

One of my friends introduced me to the custom's office as Tali Man (Tali Man was a person who had to count the goods that were going to be carried on a ship).

They asked me to give them the military service exemption card, which I didn't have. Unemployed and not having money was annoying me. I decided to start construction work until I found a better job in another field. At home, I had a free English class. In prison, I had passed an intensive English course. Ostad Mohammad accepted me to go to construction work with him. He was a plasterer. I started to learn this job from him. We had an Armenian neighbour named Serkis, who had been arrested for a short time back when he was a university student. And when he realised I was unemployed, he called me and said don't worry, he would find me a job. Mr. Serkis was a contractor of Hadish Construction Company. (Hadish company oversaw all the construction work of the Navy, a branch of that company was in Bushehr as well and it belonged to Pahlavan, the Shah's cousin. And forty percent of its share belonged to an Israeli company). After few days, he said that he had found a job in the employment sector of the company for me. He said to go to Mohsen Falahvand. Mr Falahvand was from Tabriz, a fired commando who had a very fit body, and his brother was head of a Bushehr police, and he was very violent. I asked Khodakhast to take me to the company; he accepted, and I went to the Hadish Company and went to Mr Fallahvand. He shook hands with me and looked at me carefully and said while smiling, "Is it you"? I said yes and asked why. He asked how much English I knew, and I said a little. He asked some questions in English; it turned out that my English was even better than his. He said they had some employees and engineers who speak English, and it's better that I speak in English a little. Anyway, I was accepted.

He introduced me to Vaziri, who seemd to be the accountant for the company, but in reality, he was the head of the company. After introducing myself to Mr Vaziri, his only question was I knew Mr Serkis?

I said he was our neighbour, and after asking some normal questions, I was hired. I

He gave me some information about working there and showed me the room where the files were kept and told me that I had to fix the files. So I was going to start working there from the next day. He also told me every day at 6 a.m., a Peikan car wouldpick me up and bring me to the company with four other employees. The working hours were from 7a.m. to noon and 2-6 p.m. On the first, I put on formal clothes, and I went to the street waiting for the Peikan, and a driver named Abbas, who was from Abade, picked me up, and on the way, he also picked up three other employees, and we went to the company.

It was a good start, and it was also a good opportunity for me to be in touch with workers and get to know more about their lifestyle.

There were Turk, Kurd, and Lor workers in the company; all of them used to live in the company, and would work in different fields. Turks were mostly bricklayers, and their job couldn't be done by others; normal workers were mostly among Kurds and Lors. There were a lot of villagers of Bushehr, among them there were some who used to live in the company, and Thursday evenings they would be sent to their villages for free; and some of them would go back to their villages every afternoon after work, and they would come back again to work the next morning for free. Most of them were farmers, and after 1341(1962), they had lost their fields and had come to Bushehr to work. They used to live in Kapar Abad, they would stay in the company at noon, but at night, they would go back to their homes. Many teenagers were also working there. Most of them had come to Bushehr with their father from different cities of Iran to work there. One of my duties that Mr Fallahvand had asked me to do was fixing all workers' files and making a good archive from them, which was a good chance for me to get to know the workers more.

Another thing that I was supposed to do was stamp workers' card and give it to them. ;. Back then, I realised that no contract had been signed with workers, and most didn't have insurance. Over there, I got to know Amrollahm who was Allah Gholi's friend; he used to work in architectural drawing, and he had been in prison in Isfahan for some time. The janitor was from the Zolm Abad neighbourhood, and he knew my family and me; he would bring tea almost every hour. Once I asked him not to do so because I thought it was hard for him to bring tea every hour. I told him I would let him know what to bring it to me. In the accounting sector, I got to know a close friend of Shokrollah Paknezhad. He was from Dezful and would always admire Shokrollah. I heard that a man worked in the warehouse who used to listen to Dariush(a famous Iranian singer) songs so loud. I went to him. I realised that he had been released from Ahvaz prison recently, and we had lots of prison friends in common.

One day, I was informed that a person named Rostami, a foreman of one of the units, had his hand stuck in one of the water pumps, and his hand was cut off. The driver of the company and I went there quickly and took him to the atomic hospital of Bushehr, which was well know as Hokhito. Without Mr Vaziri's permission, I filled a form that confirmed the incident report and gave it to the hospital, and I sent a copy to the office of the company where I used to work. Mr Vaziri got so angry, and the company was forced to send him to Israel for treatment. Fallahvand and Vaziri were so angry that I had filed the incident report without asking for their permission, Fallahvand said I wasn't allowed to do it, and I should lose my job.

But nothing happened, and I continued there. After that day, once Mr Ghafouri, the company's cashier, came to our unit and was happy that I had written and confirmed that form.

Hadish company was building four 15-floors building, and several times, some people had been thrown down through the elevator holes. The company had not reported those incidents at all, and they had written the incident form report in a way that the workers were in charge of the incident, and they didn't have any insurance at all. As a result, the company authorities didn't need to do anything special for those workers. Once, when I went to the company, the janitor said Naser, one of the teenagers who used to work for the company, had thrown down from the 15th floor through the elevator hole, and he had died. I quickly went to the 15th floor, but they had ended the story by giving his father some items not to let him protest. This event happened in Mordad, 1356 (August 10, 1977) I reported the incident to the Keihan newspaper, but they didn't let the Keihan's reporter enter the company. Vaziri was so angry and was looking to find who had reported to them.

One day, when I was copying in the photocopy room, Safaei, the second deputy of accounting unit, saw me and said to be aware not to use this photocopy machine for any other purpose! I was wondering what he was talking about. I asked what he meant. He asked if I had been in prison, and I said yes! He answered that they don't like anti-government people. I went back to the office and to the accounting unit and shared what happened with Mr Ghafouri. He said to be careful. Safaei was a mischievous, deceitful person, who was most probably working for SAVAK. Stay away from him. He is too dangerous. In the morning, if I couldn't get to the company's Peikan in time, some Israeli works and engineers who knew me would take me. In the muggy weather of Bushehr, what they would do was so admirable. Once after noon when we came out of the company to a hot sunny day, Mr Fallahvand, two other employees, and I got on the Peikan car that belonged to the company (that day the driver was Abbas Bachezade, and he had picked me up several times by then), and we went towards home. He dropped off other employees on the way like always, but suddenly, he changed his way. I argued that he was going in the wrong direction, and I said he should drop me off sooner than Fallahvand. He didn't care at all and just continued his way until we got to Fallahvand's house. Mr Fallahvand invited me into his home. I said thanks, but I prefered to go to home. I asked Abbas to take me home. He started to laugh, and he said it was late and I should get off the car right there. He didn't even listen to Mr Fallahvand, and said I hate anti-Shah people. It was not acceptable at all to behave like that. I again asked him to take me home, but he made fun of me. I became so angry. I got off the car and went towards him and punched him in the face several times and ran away from that scene. I went to the beach and swam in the sea. I ate food at the beach and in the evening, I went back home.

I got to my neighbourhood at 6 p.m. As I got close to our alley, some guys came to me and said not to go home! Your home is full of guards. I said I would go there; I'm not afraid of them. I went straight home. Some jeeps of the gendarmerie were parked in front of our house. As soon as I entered the house, the guards attacked me and laid me on the ground and handcuffed me. They started to search me and our home as well. After that, they took me to the police station number 2, which was close to our home by their jeep.

As soon as I entered the police station, some guards knew me, and they wondered why I was there once again. I entered the guard's officer room. Officer guard was a young man. He said it has been reported that I had a fight.

Allahverdi, a representative of workers and secret agent of SAVAK in the company, Kermanshahi, and also Abbas as plaintiffs were there. I explained the story, I said Mr Fallahvand was also there, and he can confirm all. Abbas kept saying that I was lying.

After my words, the officer guard said I should spend tonight in solitary confinement, and tomorrow, he would decide about me. I unbuckled my pant belt, and I put it on the table and said I'm ready for it. The officer looked at me before asking his next question. I said I was released from Adel Abad prison just recently, and I just defended myself.

The telephone rang, it was SAVAK. They asked the officer to send me there. The guard officer looked at me and said that SAVAK wanted me, and they should give me to them. I said no problem. I have not committed a crime to be afraid of SAVAK. After that, once again, the telephone rang, and this time, they talked with Allahverdi for a while. I was waiting to be either sent to solitary confinement or SAVAK. After some minutes, the telephone rang again, and the guard officer spoke to someone on the phone who had a higher rank and kept saying yes sure! After the phone call, the guard officer said I was free to go home. Abbas was wondering what was going on. I picked my belt and came out of the guard officer's room. The guards who had arrested me violently were looking at me wondering what happened. I just thanked some of the guards who I knew in that police station, and I left. I saw my mom was waiting in front of the police station, and we went home. So, once again, I had to find a new job. Maybe, once again, I had to go to work with Ostad Mohammad who was a plasterer. In the morning, Khodakhast took me to the company and asked if I wanted him to wait. I said no thanks; I will come back on my own. The guard recognised me and said not to go in. People from Abade gathered, and they wanted to beat me. I said no problem; I'm not afraid of them. I went to the recruitment office. Over there I saw that some people were waiting for me in front of one of the buildings. Abbas' cousin came and wanted to start the fight. I explained to him what happened and the fact that he had insulted me. Amrollah, Allah Gholi's friend, quickly came out of his room, and we talked a bit. He talked with Abbas' cousin and after some minutes, all things were normal and nothing happened. I went to the recruitment office and sat at my desk. Mr Vaziri called me to his office after some minutes. I went to his office and his wife, Mrs Nobari, who was his deputy, was there as well. Mrs Nobari was sister of Hamidreza Nobari, who became Governor of the Central Bank of Iran after the revolution. He asked me to sit. First, he spoke for few minutes and said we saboteurs only fight with lower class people and can do nothing special. Just in the streets you assassinate some patriot officers. I just listened and stayed quiet. After his words, I took off my watch and put it in my pocket, and I told him that I have learned to defend myself, and I won't let anybody disrespect me, and I became aggressive. I felt like his wife was scared, and Vaziri as well. I stood and said I won't stay anymore! I left the room in an angry way. I went straight to Ghafouri, and I told him what happened. He was cashier of the company and had enough information about all processes in the company and told me most probably within some minutes they will send an official letter here to fire me from the company. He said to stay there until I get the order to give me my salary for the days that I worked. I said okay, thanks, so until then, I went to the recruitment office to meet Mr Fallahvand and tell him the story as well and also to give back the keys, then I would be back. The janitor came to me quickly and asked what happened. I explained the whole story. I waited for some minutes, but no letter was sent to fire me.

I told Mr Ghafouri that I would be back in upcoming days to get my salary, and I left the company. I got on a bus and went back home. I was thinking of finding a new job. I had a little saving as well. I had to keep fighting. I had come back from somewhere people had sacrificed due to human ideals and I had learned the way of fighting from them. I knew one way to make a connection with the Organisation abroad, and I had heard in prison that after 1355(1976) the situation had become hard, and the best way to make a connection with the Organisation was through Palestinian organisations, and I was thinking about going to Palestine, and after what happened to me, I became more determined.

During those days, I had also saved some money. We had an acquaintance who was a captain and had a launch boat. I decided to meet him and check all details with him to go to Kuwait illegally if I could. As Al-Fath had an important base in Kuwait. But first, I tried to apply for a passport. If they gave me passport, it would be easier for me to leave, otherwise, I would leave the country illegally.

DECIDING TO LEAVE THE COUNTRY

One day in the morning, I decided to go to the passport office. I had also taken the deprivation card with me. When I entered the office, I came across one of our relatives I was happy, and I considered it a positive sign. I went to his desk, and after greeting, he asked why I was there. I said I came to get a passport. He laughed and said I need edthese particular documents for a visa. I said I didn't have a military service card, but I had a deprivation card. He wondered and asked me to show him my card. He took it and looked. I explained I was in prison more than two years, and they gave me the card. He took the card to the passport officer to ask about the situation. The officer then asked me to go to him. I again explained for him, and I said according to this card, I'm deprived from social rights for 10 years. He told me in a friendly way that they won't give me a passport and don't waste my energy. I got my card and went back home. The government had closed all doors on life for me.

This time, I decided to find our acquaintance who owned a launch boat. I found him with difficulties as I had to be cautious as some smugglers would inform SAVAK of those who wanted to leave the country illegally, and specifically, if they knew that I had just been released recently. When I went to him, he was happy. We were almost the same age, so we could easily understand each other; he said he was sorry that he had not been able to come see me as he had been abroad during recent times. I said I was going to Bahrain. I would come to him before my trip. That was a good opportunity for me. After some days, he came to our house, and we had lunch together; soon afterwards, we went for a walk. We talked about almost everything during our talks. I tried to make him talk about going to European countries several times. He answered my questions with caution. Finally, I asked him if I wanted to leave the country illegally to Kuwait, how much would it cost. He said Kuwait had changed, and it was hard to find a job there.

Kuwait had strict rules. And atheir currency Kuwaiti dinar is worthless against our currency Rial. I said I want to go to Palestine as Iraq is not safe, and it's so hard to get there these days. It's easier for me to go to Kuwait. He said after my trip to Bahrain, I would go to Kuwait and in that trip, I would get more information about it. Of course, for me, the trip would be for free. I said I know that in Kuwait there is a big Palestinian base. I became so hopeful about the future. I didn't have to pay, and he was so trustworthy. One evening when I went back home, I met a woman who had been freed from prison recently.

She was one of the arrested members of the so- called People's Liberation Organization, known as the Sirus Nahavandi Organization. She and one of her friends were among those arrested during the mass arrests by SAVAK in 1355(1976). When I was in ward four, I had heard that two Bushehri women were also upstairs. I was so happy and we talked a little bit about her arrest and the point that she was supposed to get back to work as a teacher; she was so happy. Every now and then, she would come our home and we would talk about different things, and we would also exchange different news.

One day, Mr Serkis came home and said he was abroad, and he had come back just recently. He had been informed that I wouldn't go to the company anymore. He said in a friendly way that I had the battlefield wrong, and hit him so bad. I explained the whole story to him. He said most probably Safaei was behind what Abbas did. He asked if I got my salary from the company, and I said no! After talking with Mr Vaziri, I left the company and didn't go there anymore. He said tomorrow we would go to the company together, and we would talk with him and try to be calm when we were in his office. He said to apologise if it was needed. I said I didn't do a wrong thing, and it was just due defending myself.

The following day, in the morning, we went to the company. I said to let me go meet with Ghafouri and Mr Fallahvand before going to Mr.Vaziri. He said that was fine, and after that, go to the janitor's room and we would go to see him together. I wanted to meet them as I wanted to realise what had happened in the company after that day.

I entered the recruitment unit. Mr Fallahvand greeted me in a friendly way and said Safaei was behind the whole story for sure, not

Abbas. I went to the janitor, and I talked for a while with them until Mr Serkis came.

Serkis started the conversation with Vaziri and joked and laughed. I sat at the corner of the room looking at these two! Vaziri didn't even answer me greeting him. I felt like that was disrespectful. I was immersed in my thoughts that Mr Serkis called me, and I went to them and stood in front of Vaziri's desk. Serkis started to explain about the fight between Abbas and me. Vaziri once again, without caring about what he had just heard from Mr Serkis said I hit one of their hardworking workers without reason. Serkis tried to make him laugh and change the atmosphere and tried to say that it had been just a personal dispute between two people and asked when I should go to the recruitment office and start my job again. Once again, I explained completely and said one of the factors was hot weather of Bushehr, and I said honestly, I'm sad for what happened, and I was looking for an opportunity to apologise to Abbas. I said if he would let me, I would go to him and apologise and I apologized that I had left his office angrily. Vaziri asked if I got money. I said no. I left the company. He accepted my apology and gave me my job back. I thanked them and left his office and went to the recruitment office. Mr Fallahvand was waiting to see what happened. I said I was back to work. He hugged me and was happy that I was going to work there once again.

I started my job again, but this time, I stamped some blank company cards, and I hid them in the home and also I would also stay in the company at noon, and I wouldn't go home and would eat lunch at the company so I could become friends with workers in different units.

Ashura night (a religious night in Iran), I was told that a political tract had been distributed in the city, and I tried to get in touch with those who had distributed them, but I didn't know where to start from and how to find them.

Ashura morning, Maryam came home, and we all went to one of our relatives' home, which was in the Zolm Abad neighbourhood, who were making Nazri food (foods cooked during religious occasions and get distributed for free among all people). On our way, I asked Maryam cautiously about the pamphlets from the night before. She said with a smile she heard about it; she was trying to say that it was them who had done it. That was a beginning point for me to get closer to Maryam to make connections with the Organisation through her, and that was a beginning point for a much more serious relationship between us.

We would meet each other two or three times during the week, and we would talk about different issues. Maryam also said that some people were eager for political activities.

FORMATION OF THE FIRST PRO-FADAEI GUERRILLA ORGANIZATION IN BUSHEHR

I made a connection with one of the prisoners who had been freed recently. He was eager to do political activities too. The question was how to start? I went to Shiraz, and after that, I went to its university and met some of those who we were in prison together in the hope of making connection with the Organisation. I rented a house that the landlord had divided into two parts, so he had a house to lend. I rented that house with my Hadish employee card, so it became easier for us in our group to meet each other. Another friend of mine was also always in the home. During this time, we had got access to some books and tracts, and we had hidden all of them in the house. One day when Maryam was in the home and we were going through a book together, the landlord showed up and knocked on the door. He entered the home angrily and saw Maryam and started shouting at me about her being there. I explained that she was my fiancée and we were going to get married. He wasn't convinced, so he asked me to give him my ID card as well, in addition to my employee card that I had already given to him, and I gave him an identity certificate from the Hadish Company that was available in the recruitment sector. Back then, one of the rules of the company was that workers had to show their identity certificate to the company while they were working there, and we would keep them in their files. I had also made an employee card with that name for myself beforehand, and with help from that friend of mine, we also made a stamp that we stamped it on the picture of the identity certificate. I showed that to the landlord and the issue was solved, but he said that I needed to vacate the house as soon as possible and, we did as we were afraid of getting in new trouble and being arrested. We rented a room in the Airport neighbourhood; luckily, the landlord of the new house was not hard on us, and we could easily gather every now and then.

During those days, we had made a connection with a man who used to live in Mashhad, and through him, we could have access to many books and pamphlets, and we started to go through them, specially those related to the Bijan Jozei political line. And we started to recognise those who could be added to us as well. We also considered our friend in Ahwaz as a trustworthy person to be added to our group.

During that time, I had formed a close relationship with the workers in the company and as the representative of the workers, Allah Verdi, had a close relationship with SAVAK. I had to be more cautious about the whole thing. In fact, Allah Verdi was the representative of the contractor more than the workers. I had to go to the labour office several times to solve the workers' problems, so I had become familiar with their typical procedures. Sometimes, I had to go to the Social Security Administration as well. For some workers, the contractor would confirm and provide them with insurance. I would fill in the insurance forms and submit them to the insurance office, which had led me to become familiar with social the insurance administration.

After going through workers' files, I realised that most didn't have insurance, and one day when I had gone to the social security administration, I shared this issue with one of my friends working there; and I said they don't provide most workers with insurance and only limited numbers of them have insurance. He said whenever it was appropriate to let them know and they would come to the company to check all files.

One day, Mr Vaziri and his wife took a few days off to go to Tehran, which was a good opportunity for me to ask the social insurance agents to come to the company. One day, early in the morning, two Social Security officers entered the recruitment room. I knew them and I had divided files into two groups beforehand; the files for workers who had been provided with insurance and the other group for those who didn't have insurance, and I gave them files for the second group. Those belonged to workers who had no insurance. They made a complete list of their names, thanked me, and left. When Mr Vaziri came back from Tehran, he asked me to go to his office to explain everything in detail; he was mad. For solving the issue, the company asked for help from Pahlevan, who was Shah's cousin, so they didn't face any problems at all, and they just said that those workers had been fired and the issue was solved; I couldn't do anything more. After some time, I suggested to Mr Vaziri that we could hold a class for illiterate workers as most of them were illiterate and said we could provide them a special bus to take them home after their class. I called the Fighting Illiteracy Organisation of Bushehr; their authorities were happy, and they invited me to their office. Over there, I met an officer, and after talking with him for a while, I realised he was interested in the Tudeh Party. We agreed to set some short-term internship classes for me to become familiar with the right teaching methods to start holding classes at the company.

I talked with Mr Vaziri. He didn't really like this idea, but his wife, who liked this idea, persuaded him to accept it. She told me to find a class in the company, and in the afternoons after working hours, start the class; of course, for free and not to consider it as overtime, and I simply accepted.

First,we tried to start from workers who used to live at the company, and after that, getting to those who used to live outside the company.

My Ahvazi friend also said that he was eager to help us. He was teacher in Ab Pakhsh village before being arrested (Ab Pakhsh was a city around Bushehr and was full of great palm trees). I also used Maryam's experience as she was already a teacher. We held two classes. One by me and another one by my friend. After a long negotiation with Mr Vaziri, he also accepted our new idea, which was holding class for some young workers from Ab Pakhsh and Dorahi villages, providing they could end their work thirty minutes earlier and also a bus that could take them back to their village. Mrs Nobari played an important role once again in making her husband accept our new idea. My Ahvazi friend was responsible for holding that class as well.

On the other hand, the workers didn't accept taking part in the classes, so we couldn't make it happen in reality. After a strike and an intensive conflict that occurred on Khark Island between workers and the authorities of the Hadish Company that led to breaking windows of Hadish's administrative offices, they closed our class as well. But I would go to insurance and recruitment offices regularly as the workers' representative, but in reality, Allah Verdi was workers representative. But workers would prefer to share their problems with me. During that time, I would hold the classes, and I would usually stay at the company to talk workers about their problems and try to find solutions to solve them. The officer in the fighting illiteracy suggested buying a video projector to play movies for workers in the afternoon. We got to do that twice, but Mr Vaziri didn't want to continue it. During this time, we had make a one-way connection with the Organisation. At the same time, we continued our studies. Still, I was thinking to find a way to leave the country and go to Palestine, and also I was worried about SAVAK and their traps. Because in our small group, we had all been freed from prison, and SAVAK would always try to keep an eye on the prisoners who had been freed.

We had lots of experiences about these issues such as Sirus Nahavandi, Abbasali Shahriari, who was well known as a man of a thousand faces; the Fadaei Organisation had successfully recognised his real identity, and he was killed later on by People's Fadaei Guerillas Organisation on 4th Esfand, 1353 (Februry 23, 1975)

The new strategy of SAVAK was benefiting from spies in different organisations, exactly how they recognised most members of Mujahedin Organisation; they would wait for a long time until recognising all members. Afterwards, they would attack; this was one of the things that I was worried about as well no t to end up in the same trap. I had made wide connections with various people by then, and I would always try to be part of the society as I considered people as the best supporters. We were also looking for a way to buy weapons, not because of attacking, just as means of self defence. We got a pistol, and we tried practice shooting, but unfortunately, that pistol was so old and didn't work at all. So we tried to get another one. We tried to use experiences of various organisations that we had gained while serving our prison sentence. We received Sad Sale (means 100 years) by Bijan Jozei; following that, we also got to go through the book "The King as the Gendarme of Imperialism" and we started to study it. I went to Shiraz several times in the hope of finding a connection within the Organisation, which was so difficult. We moved to a new house in Shiraz. For the first time, we also bought a typing machine and a photocopier that had a function for copying photos as well by using special paper. It had two types of yellow and green paper that we used to type on—we had to change the yellow one after copying some papers to use the green—it was such a difficult process, but it was worth it. By using a special strategy, we bought lots of papers at once, which decreased the risk of getting caught by going to the shop several times in a month.

Everything was ready for creating a new team and asserting it as a new group, and we succeeded to find the guys who had distributed the political pamphlets in Ashura night(a religious night in Iran). I went to some people with caution, but I couldn't get the appropriate answer that I was looking for. We continued on our way; our focus was on labour issues.

Maryam and I would meet more often; there was chemistry between us. Due to those days special situations, we didn't express our love. We kept studying; everything was ready to announce. During this time, Mr Vaziri took a leave and his brother-in-law took over the responsibilities temporarily. In my free time, I would study English in the recruitment office.

One day, Alireza Nobari, Mrs. Nobari's brother, came to our room and saw that I was studying a book. He asked what I was doing. I said studying English! He asked why. Do you want to go to university? I said no. I'd like to learn English to go through the books that I'm interested in, in their original language. He said asked of I had been in prison. I said I was arrested when I was a student in high school, and I was in prison for two and half years. After some days, he invited me to his home; and during the discussions we had, it became clear that he was interested in the Liberation Organisation political ideology. One night, he asked if I knew Mr Vaziri? I said no! I just knew that he was head of the company accounting sector and the official representative of Mr. Pahlevan.! He said that he was brother of Colonel Vaziri, head of Evin prison in Tehran. I was surprised because the name of Colonel Vaziri in Evin was associated with torture and violence in prison. I said so that's why that after my fight with Abbas, I was released when by single call from Mr. Vaziri (Colonel Vaziri the head of Evin Prison after he and Colonel Zibaei had tortured lots of people after the 1332 (1954) coup, and his presence in the Joint Committee was always meant beating prisoners during the massacre of 31.1.1354 (April20, 1975) that nine prisoners were executed on Evin Hill. He was in charge of the operation.) Mr Nobari said that Vaziri was in Germany now as Colonel Vaziri was dying. During this time, a theatre was staged, directed by Mr Faghih. Maryam also came, and we three went to that theatre, and after that, he introduced me to Mr Faghih. During that time, we had become so close to each other. I told him they wouldn't issue me passport, and I would try to leave the country somehow. He said maybe he could help to find a way to go abroad. He gave me his home phone number in Tehran. He said to call him if there was something he could help with. A few days later, Mr Vaziri returned from leave; he was wearing a black shirt! His brother, Colonel Vaziri, had died.

All the employees of the company went to him to offer their condolences, except me. I did not want to. The year 1977 was Sadat's trip to Israel; all Israelis celebrated, and all the company's employees were invited to the celebration, but I said that I was not willing to go. The celebration took place in the large drawing hall. One or two Israeli engineers came to me. They knew me and invited me to the party. Because I defended the people of Palestine, I could not celebrate this betrayal of Anwar Sadat to the people of Palestine. And after the celebration, the head of the company, who was an Israeli engineer, came to me and asked about my absence in the celebration in Persian and English.

I explained that I did not attend the celebration because I defended the Palestinian people. One of the Israeli engineers who would usually pick me up on his way to the company also asked me why I was not at the celebration, and I explained it to him.

In any case, it ended the same way.

Meanwhile, in the Keyhan newspaper, I read the report of the US Congress, which had mentioned the name of the Fadaiyan and Mujahedin organizations.

At the company, I would try to solve workers issues as much as I could, and I was thinking of becoming the representative of workers to defend their rights.

At the same time, I kept studying, and we distributed our first tracts on the occasion of the 19th of Bahman (February)(in the name of sympathizers of the Bushehr branch of the Fadaei Khalgh guerrillas).

We couldn't print numerous pamphlets as we had some limitations, so we would only distribute them to houses that we had chosen beforehand, those items were considered as our existing announcement.

We started to type the book, Tarikhe Sad Sale (means history of hundred years history) by Bijan Jozei; of course again in limited numbers. Once there was a picture of Shah shooting a pistol on the front page of the Keihan newspaper. I put anew on it, "Who is this dictator shooting at"? and we distributed it in the city. During a football match between the Bushehr team and veteran workers' football team of a German company, we again distributed some other pamphlets there as well. Following that, we received some books and pamphlets signed by the Guerrillas Organisation, and we decided to copy and distribute them. We also tried to make connections with more people. I would spend some time in the recruitment office as well as the labour office. Back then, I realised there was a big corruption in the Labour Department, and I reported it to our group, and we decided to explode the Labour Department if possible, and we were capable of doing so. We decided to gather more information about there and set it on fire when possible, but it was later cancelled. The company's janitor used to live there with his family, which would make it too risky to keep to our plans. One day, my Ahvazi friend came to me and said that he had found a job with the Hakhito Company. (it was the German Atomic company working in Bushehr.) He said he would send his new address after finding a house there, and after that, we could continue our activities once again. After some days, I went to the company, and I met him. He stayed in the workers' dormitory of the company and could stay in touch with workers. We tried to make a new group inside the company as well. On one hand, this atomic company was huge, and it had lots of workers and also there were a lot of workers and engineers from the Soviet Socialist country working there. But it was so hard to get in touch with them as they couldn't speak in English, but we did our best to do so. In this company, exactly like the Hadish Company, most Iranian workers were from Bushehr's villages. Following that, we made a connection in the Tesa Company as well (Tesa was an American company that was in charge of the Airforce needs). We had already made great connections.

We had also made a good connection with a person at the Saadat high school; during this time, I would go to Shiraz a lot to become more knowledgeable in politics and to increase the group's political knowledge level. We were working on Bijan Jozei books, but it would take a lot of time as we had limited facilities available. I decided to use the company's photocopier, which was hell risky, specially considering that the photocopy machine was under control of Safaei. I had to pass by his room to get to the photocopy room, and he would always get in the room after some minutes, which made it difficult to keep to that plan, and above all, it was said that if we use the photocopy machine, SAVAK will become aware of it.

MARRIAGE AND POLITICAL WORK

My relationship with Maryam could be trouble because in those days, it was difficult for Maryam to come to the home that we had rented so we would usually meet each other in my mother's house, which was not safe either.

As she had been arrested in the past, Bushehr's traditions had made it difficult for us to stay in touch easily. Above all, there was chemistry between us. After some time, I proposed to Maryam. I said this way she would be freer, and we could rent a house easier, and in case of going on a trip, we wouldn't face any problem. Hotels wouldn't let men and women who were not married stay in a same room. Once SAVAK had asked Maryam's father to go to SAVAK, and they had warned him about Maryam's relationship with me, which hastened my proposing. Some changes had occurred in SAVAK as well. Iravani, who was very violent, had been transferred and a person whose name was Davoudi had become head of SAVAK in our city, who was not a rough man. Maryam's family would control her more; they didn't want her to meet me anymore.

Despite all these difficulties, we continued meeting each other, discussing the books that we would go through, which helped me to propose to Maryam, and finally, she accepted. It was common to take some gold jewellery to a woman's house while proposing. I thought how to solve this issue. One of my friends said he would give me my brother's wife jewelleries, but I should give it back to her after that occasion. Maryam's family wouldn't accept it as her father was under SAVAK's pressure as well. Maryam did her best to make them accept me; her independent personality played an important role in making them accept me. The night we went to their home for proposing, her father said the marriage was suspicious, and he hoped you two are telling the truth, and Maryam said firmly we would get married. Her father was summoned to SAVAK once again, and they told him he shouldn't let the marriage take place; otherwise, we'd be killed. As a result, her father tried not to let us get married, but he couldn't stop us.

One of our conditions was neither taking pictures nor playing music, as after the Tabriz conflict, people were mourning, Shah had killed people due to anti-government protests. I I had a few Afghani friends who came to perform soft music.

I had invited few people; Maryam's family had invited Mr Vaziri too; her family knew him because of trading iron together. We ended our wedding night with an Afghani song and all guests liked it. After our marriage, SAVAK summoned Maryam's father once again. We rented a room, and we moved to our new house. We got married on 4.12.1356 (February 23, 1978), and soon afterwards, we went to Shiraz and found our old friends. After coming back to Bushehr, Mr Nobari was back once again. I was happy; he invited us to his home, which was Mr Vaziri's home. He said Mr Vaziri had taken some time off, and he said he had a wedding gift for me. I said we tried not to get gifts from anybody, and we were on vacation as Mr Vaziri had given us some days off through Maryam's uncle. We discussed a lot about social and political events that night. We met an American newswriter in his home who was Mr Nobari's friend. He explained that he had interviewed Bazargan and Dr Sahabi. He was interested in visiting and making a report about southern regions. Mr Nobari would translate his words. He was curious to know about the prison's situation as well, so he asked us some questions about it. He showed us the list of political prisoners published by Amnesty International; I knew some of them and explained to him. He gave us a magazine with a picture of Shah and Carter in, crying because American police were firing tear gas at students while protesting. Mr Nobari told me if I went to Tehran to call him. The night after that, I gave a pamphlet of The Sympathy of the People's Fedayeen Guerrilla Organization to the newswriter. We also distributed some pamphlets about boycotting the Nowruz and buying stuff related to the occasion due to massacre of people by Shah and the inflation rate. We decided to distribute those pamphlets in Borazjan. We went to that city with one of my friends, and as we were leaving the city, we got stuck in a dead end alley, but we escaped.

We started to copy one of the Organisations pamphlets, and as usual, we distributed them at night between the houses that we had identified beforehand. We decided also to distribute some of them on Friday in front of the cinema when it was crowded over there. We went in the morning, and it was so crowded, I called the police and said we have planned a bomb in the cinema; we wanted to distribute the pamphlets after people evacuated. Police didn't care, just few policemen came and checked the situation and left.

On Fridays, the city was usually crowded, so we took some pamphlets to distribute. I gave some of them to a child and some money, and I asked him to distribute them among people; police caught him and released him afterwards.

We needed money as we were going to buy a photo stencil. So we needed a lot of money. One of our friends said one of his relatives had a lot of women's wrist watches that were smuggled and we could confiscate them. On a rainy night, we confiscated the wrist watches and put them in a safe place. Later, we sold them and spent the money for the organisation. We typed the book Tarikh Sad Sale by Bijan Jozei and printed it in limited numbers. During this time, we would travel to Shiraz a lot; we had made lots of connections at Shiraz University with our prison friends. We helped university students, and we had become active in university the movie theatre. We used to go there a lot that even the university guard thought that we were students,and they wouldn't ask us to show them university cards. We started to take part in Shiraz protests. against Shah. I bought a Peikan with another name that we could use to travel whenever we wanted. We would go to Shiraz almost every Thursday, and we would take part in the protests at night and come back to Bushehr on Friday nights. We called some of the prisoners who had been freed.

We would take part in almost every protest. We had a relationship with religious activists as wel;l they didn't know that we were left-wing activists. We would try to change their slogans in our favour. One of our friends was arrested when doing such things and was released on bail some days after that. I was thinking about the Saderat Bank in Astane neighbourhood, and I was planning to attack the bank and steal its money. We made plan to attack there at night. We moved towards there, but we came across lots of demonstrators, so we were forced to flee.

One of my best connections was with one of my prison friends who had been transferred from Tehran to Shiraz, and he had been released from Shiraz as well. He used to work in the Shiraz municipality as an engineer. He always gave us a lot of useful information with correct analyses. After the revolution, I met him in front of the Organisation Headquarters at Tehran University; he had special card of the Organisation, and he participated in organising the Organisation Headquarters in Tabriz. But unfortunately, I can't remember his name.

We concluded that we needed to take part in the protests more actively and tried to change the slogans in our favour. One night during a strong protest in Shah Cheragh (a neighbourhood in Shiraz city), the policemen threw tear gas in the middle of the crowd, which I picked it up and ran towards the policemen, which caused a commotion. I was about to die; they washed my face with a considerable amount of water, and finally, I got better and fled from Shah Cheragh (a neighbourhood in Shiraz city) as policemen attacked, and they were looking for the one who had thrown the tear gas at them. I had made some company cards with my picture and various names in addition to a university card to have in case of being asked to show it to university guards. We had become so active in our group; our focus was on protests in Shiraz.

We also distributed several pamphlets signed by sympathizers of the Fadaei Guerrillas Organisation at the university and protests.

According to those days' situation, we gave back the room that we had rented from the landlord, and we put the stuff that we had provided in a safe place. I had a feeling that our identity had been exposed. Several times in different places we would change our way on purpose to make sure that nobody was following us.

Schools were about to be closed, which was the best opportunity for us to leave Bushehr.

Maryam was a teacher, so she could rent a room in one of Shiraz schools for free, and we had an excuse to stay there. I didn't feel safe; we thought that we were being pursued imperceptibly, and we had to be more careful. We limited our communication to make sure we were not in danger. I asked for paid leave from the company that Mr Vaziri didn't accept,but he gave me some days off. We prepared to travel to Shiraz. We also tried to sell the wrist watches to give money to the Organisation as financial aid. We went to Shiraz we had some pamphlets in our car.

We stayed in shiraz for some time during that time we would regularly take part in protests. At some point, I felt like a car was following us.

I asked Maryam to check the car as I thought we were being followed; we couldn't see them and didn't understand where they went. Because we didn't feel safe in Shiraz, we decided to go to Teran; over there, we could stay in touch with the Organisation much easier.

In Shiraz, we had some pamphlets signed by sympathizers of the Fadaei Guerrillas Organisation;we put them in our car and tried to distribute them and go to Tehran after that.

After distributing them, I realised that we were being followed. I told Maryam about it. I tried to go faster until they couldn't follow us, but I ended up with having an accident with a Peugeot. First, I wanted to run away, but I got out of the car. There was a heavy traffic jam. The driver was a young man. He got out of his car and smiled. He felt I was scared and said to calm down and asked why I was afraid. He asked if I had a driver's license. I said my problem was something else; Savak was after me. He said we could go to an automobile repair shop owned by one of his friends, and he would repair our cars. We went there together. The cars were not badly damaged. I asked how much I should I. He said I didn't need to pay, I thanked him, and we went on our way.

We went to the university at night, and we decided to leave Shiraz as soon as possible. Maryam and I and one of her friends, a Kurd woman who was in prison with Maryam, moved towards Tehran early in the morning. We stopped in Abadeh to rest and eat and then we could go directly to Tehran. There was a fast-food restaurant, and I got some sandwiches. The owner of was such a friendly man, and we became friends. We were planning to get to Tehran early in the morning as it was easier to pass police stations at that time. I had Alireza's phone number to call in case it was necessary. Before moving towards Tehran, I also informed our Kurd friend that we had hidden some reports and wrist watches in the car.

We move towards Tehran. Around Shahreza city, suddenly, my cigarette fell on my foot. I wanted to extinguish the cigarette and lost the car's control, which led to having a crash with a minibus that was coming straight to us in the other lane (I read that accident report after the revolution; it was mentioned the minibus had hit the rear fender of our car, which led the minibus to go off the road, 13 people were injured); it was a terrible accident.

The back of our car was almost destroyed. My friend and I were sitting in front and didn't get injured, but shards of the car had injured Maryam. I told our friend take everything including our documents to Shira. And we went to the Shahreza hospital by a Peikan.

When we got to the hospital, medical staff were preparing as they had already heard about the accident. Maryam was taken to the operating room soon afterwards. The hospital's guard asked me which car I was in, and I said the minibus. He laughed and said I must be wrong. The minibus was coming from Yazdkhast, and all of them were relatives (Yazdkhast was one of the Fars province cities, was located 65 km far from Shahreza and 60 km far from Abadeh. Its history goes back to Sassanids arrival). I said was a university student, and I showed my card and that we were going to Tehran. As you are student and had a terrible accident, even if police don't catch you, the people of Shahreza will kill you, and the best way is to flee.

He said as soon as my wife felt better, leave the city. I said we have got no money now. I don't have shoes on. He said not to worry. He would pay, Maryam came out of the operating room with swollen and bandaged face and bloody clothes; wounded passengers of the minibus had just been brought to hospital by private cars. I told Maryam that we had to runaway as the situation was not good. By that time, the hospital guard had also rented a black car for us. We got in the car ; we went to Shiraz. I thanked the guard and promised to give his money back on my next trip.

On the way,I could see other cars taking other wounded passengers of the minibus to the hospital. When we were passing by our own car, the driver slowed. I saw our car and realized it was such a terrible accident we had. The driver asked where we wanted to go. I thought and said either Abadeh or Shiraz.

He said the hospital guard gave him little money, so he could not take us there. He stopped the car after a while and said to get out. I said the hospital guard said he would take us at least to Abadeh. He said no.

I said it's getting dark and it's cold, and if we get out here, the wolves would tear us apart. He didn't accept and said if we didn't get out of the car, he would get back to Shahreza and give us to the police. We got out of the the car in the hope of continuing our way with another car passing by. It was getting dark, and we were shaking from cold; the driver left without worrying about us.

We were shaking from cold and hunger as I had only a crimson shirt on and Maryam a normal shirt that was thoroughly bloody. Nights in that area were so cold. A truck carrying stones appeared in the distance. I went forward and raised my hand. The truck stopped. I also noticed that when the co-driver got out, he had a wooden stick in his hand as he was afraid. As soon as he saw Maryam's bloody face and my bloody shirt, he was relieved and put the stick aside. He asked what happened. I said please take us to a city. I would be thankful, and we have no money. The driver looked at us carefully and then said to get in.

We got in the truck, and we sat in front beside the driver. His co-driver sat behind us; they behaved so friendly and humane to us.

The first question that he asked was if we were hungry. We said yes, fortunately, inside the truck warm.

The driver asked what was the matter? I said we had an accident. He said he had seen it. "Did you run away from the accident scene"? he asked. I said yes. And I'm a university student,t and I ran away as I was afraid of the police. He asked if we were anti-government. He continued that these days, all young people, specially university students, were against the government. He asked his friend to give us some bread and cheese and also hot tea to warm us. He started to listen to a song by Susan, and he didn't ask any further questions. Maryam's pain had just begun; she was moaning, and the truck driver was looking for a painkiller but couldn't find any until we git to Abadeh. I saw the fast-food restaurant that I had bought sandwiches from him, and I asked the driver to pull over. I said thanks a bunch for helping us. He said if he was going to Shiraz, for sure, he would take us.

I found a dark alley, and I told Maryam to go there and hide in the dark so nobody would see her. I said I would go to the fast-food restaurant; maybe I could borrow some money from the owner who was a friendly man. I went towards the restaurant! It seemed like it was where all young people of Abadeh would gather. It was so crowded everyone was young. As I was getting close to the restaurant, I could hear that they were all talking about the accident, and they were saying that the driver and other passengers ran away. I entered the restaurant with a bloody shirt and no shoes. All the people were staring at me. I went directly to the owner of the restaurant. He was a fat man. We had bought the sandwiches from him in the morning, and three of us had joked and laughed a little bit with him. I asked if he remembered the morning. He looked at me suspiciously and said maybe. I said I need one hundred tomans to get to Shiraz. And I pledged a watch to him. I said I would pay him back when I got back, you he could have my watch until then.

He said they don't give money to people and to go somewhere else. I said I bought sandwiches from him this morning. He answered he didn't remember.

A skinny young guy looked at me and asked what the problem was. I said I needed onehundred toman to go to Shiraz! He asked why I was bloody "What are you doing here"? he asked. I said I was a university student and showed him my card. He said I didn't need to show that and asked what I wanted. I again said one hundred tomans to get to Shiraz, and I will give you my university card and my watch to make you sure I will pay you back. He said he recommended I stay in this city tonight and leave tomorrow. I said no thanks.

He asked if I was the driver of the Peikan in the accident. I said yes. He asked if I ran away from the scene. I said yes. He asked why. I said I was so tired and exhausted that I didn't feel like talking more about it; by then, young people had gathered around us.

He ordered a sandwich, and I said there were two of us, and he ordered another one. We left the restaurant. Maryam was hiding in the darkness of the alley. We went to her. We talked for a while. He said we needed to go to the hospital to check her wounds, so we all went to the hospital. A nurse came who knew that man they talked a little bit. Later on, he said wait for him and he would be back when the nurse changed her bandages. At first, I doubted, but I told myself I didn't care what would happen, I was just worried about Maryam. He came back after a while and brought a pair of shoes and a shirt for me.

I changed my shirt. Maryam's clothes were bloody, but we couldn't do anything about it. After changing the dressing, he asked us to go to his home to rest and leave tomorrow. I said we should go. He said okay so take a taxi to Shiraz. A car was there looking for passengers to go to Shiraz. He went to the driver and talked with him and paid the fare and gave me some money not to get in trouble in Shiraz.

We thanked him. Maryam went to the back seat in the dark, not to be seen by the driver. I gave him my university card, and I wanted to give him my wristwatch but he wouldn't take it. I asked for his address to pay him back next time, and he gave me his address. We said goodbye, and I got in the car, and we waited to move to Shiraz. Some other passengers came, and the Peikan car started to go to Shiraz. On the way, passengers were talking about the accident; any of them had a different opinion about it, I was listening, and Maryam was sleeping as she had taken a strong painkiller at the hospital. I was aware not to get involved in their discussion. They were saying that there had been three people in the car accident, two women and a man, one of the women had fled from the accident scene, and two others had ran away from the hospital. (Abadeh is the northernmost city of Fars. And the natives of this city speak Persian and with an Abadei accent. The pastures of this city have long been the summer camps of different Qashqai tribes. Many of Qashqais had started to in Abadeh and the surrounding cities; people of the city were so friendly and hospitable.)

Shiraz was four hours from Abadeh, and we git to Shiraz at two after midnight. We got off at Darvaze Quran (means Quran door), a famous place in Shiraz, and we waited for another taxi to go inside the city. We got in a small car. He asked me where to go, and I showed him the way.

After a while, we realised he was gendarme as as his special cap was in the car.

He explained that during days he worked as a gendarme, and at nights, he work as a taxi driver due to financial problems to be able to afford his life. Again, in his car, there was a discussion about the accident and the point that they had run away and the rumour reached the point that policemen were following them, and after the accident, they had fled from the accident scene.

Maryam had a university friend who had a room on Shahpur Street behind Karim Khan Arg. We got off in the Shahrdari Boulevard, and after some minutes and making sure that no one was following us, we went to her friend's room.

There were some male and female students there; they were all looking at us in horror and were waiting for us to explain to them. Early in the morning, Maryam went to the hospital with her friend, and we had some friends there who were doctors, and they treated her without the police.

After she came back, we went to meet our friends, and on the way, I was thinking how to solve the issue. I had got the car documents with one of my friends' identity details. I calledhim and told him the story about what happened, specially the watches that had been impounded by gendarmerie, and I asked him to come to Shiraz as soon as possible. He came to Shiraz, and he said we can make a fake cash memo to get back the watches from gendarmerie, and we could solve the accident issue in a way. Of course, we were so naive.

When it rains, it pours! I was confused and I couldn't think clearly. Anyway, after a while, we changed our clothes and appearance, and we went to few watch stores, but we couldn't get a cash memo from them. Until the moment in Vakil Bazaar, a watch store owner working in a small store agreed to give us a cash memo. He said wait for some minutes, and suddenly, a few plainclothes officers showed up and arrested us. We were not handcuffed; they held our hands tightly. Vakil Bazaar was not so far from the police station. My friend and I were taken to the police station on foot with those officers. On the way, they asked no questions.

The police station and the Joint Committee were behind Arg Karim Khan. I knew the neighbourhood a little bit. As we got close to the police station, suddenly, I freed myself from the officer and started running away. As I explained earlier, the Joint Committee was next to the police station and after passing the Committee, one could get to the main street, Zand Street, and on the right was Shiraz gendarmerie and on the left was Melli Bank. If I could get to the main street, they couldn't arrest me because I could start chanting and disappear into the crowd. But as soon as I entered the main street, I turned right to the gendarmerie by mistake; many gendarmes were standing there as there were lots of protests in the city, and they were ready.

I was arrested once again, and they took me the police station and started to beat me as they were taking me in. They took me to the room of the head gendarmerie and laid me on the floor, brought a stick, and they kept my feet above me. Two policemen grabbed the wood on both sides, and another one started to kick the sole of my foot. The head of the gendarmerie would also encourage them to continue beating me. I explained everything for them from watching the smuggling to fleeing from the accident scene. After that, they brought my friend as well, and they started to beat him. When they were beating us, I could also hear my friends' voice. They had been arrested in the protests as well. When I met them, they explained while they were protesting, police had attacked and caught them. Among them were also Maryam's friend, who was a university student. They found some political books and papers in her home, which led the officers from the story of watches smuggling to political interrogating.

Maryam was beaten as well. We spent the night in the police station, and the following day, they took us to the Administration of Justice. Over there, a photographer came and took pictures of us, and he said he works with the Keihan newspaper. We were taken back to the police station once again. They took Maryam and me to the head of the police station room, and they started to beat me. He said we communists were used to sharing everything. "You can share your wife with me now". I was beaten up. After that, Arman came in and sat on a sit in front of me. I was sitting on the floor and Maryam was standing at the corner of the room. After speaking for a while, exerting his power, he said we were there once again, and without beating or insulting us, he left the room, and we were brought to our friends. In the afternoon, they took all of us to Adel Abad prison. Six of us, Maryam and her friend who was a university student, and we four.

IN ADEL ABAD PRISON WARD ONE AND RELIGIOUS PRISONERS

When we got to the prison as usual, we had to sign some papers. The guards knew Maryam and I, and they treated us respectfully. My friends and I were taken to ward one, Maryam and her friend were taken to ward four on the third floor.

When I entered ward one, Keshvari was serving as the guard whose nickname was Reza Khan. He treated me well and gave each of us a cell and asked if I needed anything. He had changed.

Ward one was full of prisoners who had been arrested during anti-Shah protests in 1357 (1978), and almost all three floors were full of prisoners. Among them, I met Rajab Ali Taheri; we were in the same room for a while in ward four in the past. We greeted, and he asked why I was there once again, and I explained briefly to him. Mehdi Hashemi was one the of the famous prisoners there. I had heard about him when I was in ward four; they were well known as Ghahdarijan detainees.

Mehdi Hashemi a Shiite cleric and of the first founding members of the Revolutionary Guards after the revolution, was son-in-law of Hoseinali Montazeri's brother, Hoseinali Montazeri, was executer in Mehr 1366 (October 1987).

He was charged with complicity in the murder of Abul Hasan Shamsabadi. They had dumped him in a well in Ghahdarijan after killing him.

Ghahdarijan was 14 km far from Isfaha. Mehdi Hashemi was arrested in 1355 (1976) for the same crime case with Jafar Shafiei, who was a quiet mysterious person. After the revolution, he was one of the behind the scene people and at the same time of the founders of the Revolutionary Guards.

Seiied Abulhasan Shams Abadi was murdered by Mahdi Hashemi's group on 18th Farvardin 1355(April7, 1976). Ruhollah Khomeini was against him, and it was also said that he had been killed following an order from Khomeini. Mehdi Hashemi was plenipotent representative of Khomeini in Iran.

Entering us to the ward was beginning of Ramadan month, which was so difficult for us because in the ward all of them were religious, and they were all fasting, and they expected us to fast as well, which caused us to have lots of difficulties. Those who had been arrested in protests would try to insult us. Back in ward for, I had gotten used to brushing my teeth while standing in line for the toilet; they insulted me few times because of this habit. Or when I would sing the Organisations anthems in a low voice, I was ridiculed. One of these young guys who became the head of the Revolutionary Guard in Shiraz after the revolution tried to insult me to show me that we were not like them, and we couldn't get along.

I explained everything to Engineer Taheri, and I also told him in this situation, the behaviour of these people was not correct at all. Of course, Engineer Taheri was one of the best people among religious forces in prison that after revolution became the first head of the Revolutionary Guard in Fars province and also the first Kazerun's district member of parliament and also one of the main members of the Islamic Republic party. Engineer Taheri, after a little explanation regarding the movement and clergy's role, said these guys were young and unexperienced with emotions that were difficult to controlled. It was clear that Taheri was acting as the leader of those who had been arrested during protests as he divided them into groups, and all of those groups would take orders from Taheri, and boycotting us was by his order. Taheri didn't let them get close to us at all. One day, when I was walking in the yard, one of them came to me and started to walk with me. He was from Abadeh, and he asked me the reason for my arrest. He used to work in Shiraz, and he had been arrested accidentally. He said they had also arrested his friend and had beaten him in Abadeh's gendarmerie in a bad way. He said his friend had helped two wounded people in Abadeh. I was wondering how similar our cases were. But the situation that we were in didn't let me explain more because I had learned from prison that it was better not to talk about things outside the prison. He was a religious one who had not been arrested during protests. He would walk with me more. One day, I asked him what happened to his friend in Abadeh. He said I didn't really know.

I told him the story of that night and the fact that I had gotten his address and put that in my pocket when they were arresting me. I had forgotten his address was still in my pocket, and police had found it in my pocket. But they didn't ask me even one question about it.

He said his name was Samad, and he was a carpet weaver. I asked this man to thank Samad when he was freed and also ask him for forgiveness as I had not been careful, which had caused him to get in trouble. Keshavri, who had worked in prison for many years had a lot of experience with political prisoners, believed that these guys didn't know anything about politics at all. But the next government is in their hands. He would give me news about country's situation. One day, he called me and said one of the prisoners of ward four was getting out of the ward, and if I wanted, I could see him. It was Hamidreza Arzpeima who was about to be sent to Tehran. I was so happy, and he said he had gotten the news that I were in ward one. I sent a letter to the head of the prison and asked him to let Maryam and I meet each other at some time.

We would meet each other ten minutes each week under guard office of ward four. I could make a connection with ward four once again. And I would let prisoners in ward four be aware of the news that I would get in ward one. Meeting Maryam had a positive effect on me, especially since we were under pressure of religious prisoners in ward one. Engineer Taheri would always try to not let those who were arrested in protests to get in touch with us at all and would usually hold classes related to religion for them, and they were busy this way. Most of the new prisoners would get released after two or three weeks on bail. This way, Engineer Taheri could send his messages to outside of the prison.

After all the correspondence, the head of the prison finally agreed that I could borrow some books from ward four, and ward four prepared a list of books as much as possible, and that was great, and we were boycotted in ward. I noticed that after we take a bath, the religious guys would go and wash the showers and everything we had touched because they believed that those items had become dirty.

They did not let us participate in other activities and preferred to share the food among themselves.

One day, a cleric entered the ward and was warmly welcomed by Taheri, and a few days later, everyone gathered in the corridor of the ward, and that cleric somehow wanted to show his power. He came to my cell and read a letter from Dastgheib asking for the cleric's release, and he was released the next day. After the revolution, he became the head of the Shiraz Jihad Construction. This cleric used to hold congregational prayers and even invited me to pray one day, and I said that I'm a left wing activist and I do not pray, which he did not like at all, and this caused us get far from the other prisoners. Another day, another cleric named Mesbah, who was from Shiraz, gathered everyone in ward one, except us, we did not go, and he held a congregational prayer, and after the prayer, they chanted harsh slogans against the government; prisoner authorities actually did nothing. They showed us that they were in power. Again, another letter was read from Dastgheib in the corridor of the ward that he had demanded the clerk's freedom immediately, and he was released soon afterwards. Finally, they let somebody visit me; my sister was the first to come to visit. She came with Seifi, one of our relatives. My sister said the day that I were arrested, Savak attacked our home and searched it. There was a rumour in the city that I had a bomb. She added that the Kurd friend of Maryam had told them about what happened to us and about the accident. That night, my sister and one of the released prisoners, Reza, had come to Shahreza, and they heard the news of us fleeing so they had come back soon afterwards. My sister had gone to gendarmerie with Naser who was a nomadic man and got the watches from them. She consulted me; I told her give them to the Organisation, and Naser gave them to the Organisation through the links he had.

My sister also added that the car that we had the accident with was parked next to gendarmerie, but nothing had left from the car. Because my sister was in Sepah Daneshclose to Isfahan, she used to visit me regularly and during those meetings, she would give me the news. One day, she came and said we are trying to talk with bar association to go through your crime case. I also said that at the moment, SAVAK has not accepted us, and we went to the judiciary through the Intelligence Office, and the judiciary issued an arrest warrant for us. But I thought we would be tried in a military court.

In the meantime, I was trying to stay in touch with Engineer Taheri and become aware of outside news from him. The news of 17 Shahrivar and its famous massacre reached the ward. I went to Engineer Taheri and said that it would be good if I could make a move and express my sympathy to the families of the victims and disgust with the perpetrators. Taheri again emphasized that those movements were for Islam, and those people had been killed for Islam, and he added he would let you know if I could do anything.

The next day, they gathered in the yard and after the congregational prayers. They started chanting and condemning the massacre.

Taheri had organized ward one in such a way that he did not allow any of the detainees of the demonstration to approach us.

He had also managed a small group of prisoners to monitor all our movements, and some of them even would go to extremes, and they would insult us. Of course, they would mostly insult the communists and that the communists are filthy and have no place among our people.

The case of Cinema Rex happened. I went to Taheri and asked for performing a collective movement, as usual he was not interested in what I would recommend. Taheri's whole effort was to boycott us.

From time to time, when a mullah was arrested, it was a religious pleasure for one or two days because they would hold congregational prayers and chant harsh slogans, and we had to adapt to the suffocating environment that they had created for us.

Many times when we were taking shower, they would pass by the bathroom window that opened in the corridor of the prison and look angrily at us and insult and provoke. Maybe they did not mind a physical confrontation.

But it was clear that they were organized by Engineer Taheri, and by filling their time with reading the Qur'an and religious books, on the other hand, giving them addresses and telephone numbers after their release had a great influence on them.

Of course, Engineer Taheri walked with me several times and emphasized that the revolution was Islamic and that we leftists should fundamentally reconsider our ideology and that door of Islamic mercy is always open to everyone.

I wrote a letter to the head of the prison requesting to be transferred to Ward four. He called me, and I went to the guard and the deputy director of the prison was there. After greeting and cheering, he told me that I had not been questioned yet. And according to the prison law, I could not be transferred to ward four until I was interrogated. And after interrogation, the situation would be clearer; maybe I would be released. So until the interrogation, they would not take me to ward four, and I hoped to be released after the interrogation.

During this time, my relationship with Keshvari had become very good, and he would use every opportunity and call me, and I would go under the guard, and we would drink tea together. He described the difference between political prisoners and those arrested during demonstrations and believed that they didn't know anything abut politics at all, and Engineer Taheri would send them out to take part in the protests.

Of course, I was very careful not to have too much contact with him. As it was more likely that I would be accused of being an informant.

So I had to be very careful. The foundations of the imperial system were shattered.

One day, my mother's cousin, who was also a prison guard and had been guarding ward four for some time, came to the ward, called me, and I went to the guardhouse, and we talked a lot.

During one of my meetings, my sister explained that a number of demonstrators went to our house and told my mother that she should come to the protests and demand the release of the political prisoners because she currently had two political prisoners, and all the political prisoners should be freed. Keshvari had become a good friend with me, and I would talk to him regularly. Ward one was regularly filled and emptied. Crowds were arrested, came, and briefly released on bail through the judiciary, and we and the three religious men were almost always in ward one. Some time later, Keshvari brought me the Keyhan newspaper, which had a photo of my car after the accident and that the passengers of the car were on the run. This news was interesting considering that I had explained the case to him. I was still waiting to be interrogated and transferred to ward four afterwards.

It was the middle of October when one day they called me to have a trial the next day and to be ready. In the morning, according to the usual routine, after doing the legal work, we went to the military court, and it was the same interrogator who had interrogated me in 1354 (1975). But this time, he was not talking from a position of power but from a position of friendship. He asked if I had ever been in prison before, and I said yes, he interrogated me.

He opened the case and said that I was accused of having links with the People's Fedayeen Guerrilla Organization! I was surprised and protested that the accusation was completely false, and I had nothing to do with them. I was arrested due to the accident, and I didn't know those three people at all. And this crime case is not related to military court at all. Only SAVAK has connected us to these issues. We have not been interrogated in Savak, and we have been beaten and interrogated in the Intelligence Office. He said that it was the report of Bushehr SAVAK that connected me to this process. I said it was a complete lie and a false accusation. We had an accident, and we ran away because of being afraid of the people of the city who had many wounded. He asked why I didn't talk about the third person. I said that it was me and Maryam, and we did not have a third person with us. He said according to the gendarmerie report of Shahreza, there were three people. I said that's a big lie, and I did not accept any accusation. Just the accident and there was not even a word of watches. Finally, when signing the questionnaire, I wrote down below the paper that we had not committed any political crime, and we must be tried in the judiciary and in the presence of a jury. He verbally said that according to SAVAK, I was wanted. I said it's a lie. We were normally living in Bushehr, and we came to Shiraz just for our summer vacation, and theaccident happened. Again, he said Savak's report showed something else. I said I told him several times it's a lie. And according to the law, Maryam and I must be tried in a court of law. Those few others have nothing to do with our case. It is only the SAVAK conspiracy that wanted to show its power. He looked at me cleverly and said, "I think you will be freed." Don't worry. I said that the fact is that this case has nothing to do with the military court, just as when you tried me in 1354 (1975), which had nothing to do with the military court.

And he interrogated our other friends, and we all went back to prison. On the way, I told Maryam about what happened between the interrogator and me, and we returned to the prison. Maryam and her friend were taken to ward four, and we were taken to ward one. During this time, the slogan "Free political prisoner must be released" was widespread. And the chances of them granting a general amnesty were very high. On the morning of the 4th of Aban (October), Keshvari called me. I did not believe that the Shah would release the political prisoners easily. It was around 10 or 11 a.m. that, once again, Keshvari called me to see political prisoners getting released from the prison.

As I explained, ward one was quarantined and covered with a green curtain. Anyway, I pulled back the curtain and looked at the end of the corridor, where section four was. The front ward was very crowded, and a number of prisoners were standing outside, and there was no line.

They was just a gathering in front of the bar with joy and applause! After a few moments, the crowd moved to the bottom, where I shouted, and the released prisoners noticed me and became so happy, saying that we had been released.

It was unbelievable. People like Mr Ghani Blourian, Amouei, Hajri, Keimanesh, who had been in prison for many years and refused to accept a royal pardon, were now being released from prison and owed this freedom to the people's struggles. In any case, many prisoners were released. Again, I returned to ward one. Engineer Taheri came and questioned what was going on, and I explained that some prisoners in ward four were released.

Some time later, the news of the release of the second group came, and it was decided that all prisoners would be released soon. It was interesting that those who were arrested during the protests would say that we protested, but the communists would be released; they were sad about this issue. One night, they called many prisoners of ward one; they were mostly university students, to be freed.

We chanted the slogan of unity, but religious prisoners as usual would shout the main help is from god. Less than an hour later, it was reported that those who had been released from prison were being taken by car to a city in Paramount.

Near Saadi Cinema, some demonstrators attacked the car and released them. The news spread like wildfire while we knew they had been released from prison.

I HEARD THE VOICE OF YOUR REVOLUTION

....

I t was the night of the 14th of Aban that Keshvari called me and said that the Shah wanted to give me an important message. I went under the guard and waited for it to air on TV. Of course, we did not have a TV in the ward. Religious prisoners were also reluctant to ask for television. In any case, I waited for the Shah's message and the defeated face of the Shah appeared on TV, and the famous message that I heard the voice of the revolution, and he introduced himself as a Shiite Muslim and that oppression would not be repeated in country gain. It was too late. He vowed to preserve the country's territorial integrity, national unity, and the Twelver Shiite religion, and to make up for past mistakes. And that I also heard the message of your revolution, the nation of Iran.

That the government of Iran in the future will be based on the constitution, social justice, and national will and away from tyranny, oppression, and corruption. But he knew that it was too late and that the foundations of his dictatorship had been shattered.

The next day, Bahman 15 (February 6), I wrote a letter to the head of the prison requesting to be transferred to ward four. Due to the fact that I had been interrogated and according to the prison law, I had to be transferred to ward fur. In ward one, the annoying behaviours of religious prisoners had increased, and they tried to harass us as much as possible by boycotting, insulting, harassing, and talking about Halal and Haram. In the yard, several times, they tried to provoke us for fighting. They would usually hold congregational prayers in the yard that we had to get back to our cell. They would do their best to annoy us in any way possible. If we touched anything, they would say to our face do not touch them as we are considered filthy. They kept listening to Quran and other religious things aloud, which was really annoying. Early in the morning, they would say Azan and would pray in group.

And we did not dare protest. As I explained, during the distribution of breakfast, lunch, and dinner, they did not allow us to interfere and gave us our share separately, and they themselves would eat together.

All this meant that if the future government is in the hands of this faction, there will be no democracy and freedom of expression. In any case, it was the evening of, 14th Azar 1357 (December 5, 1957), when it was announced that at six or seven o'clock in the afternoon, 15 of us would be released from prison. Two women from ward, seven people from ward one, and six people from ward four were freed. We packed up and got ready for getting released. It was 8 p.m. when they called us, and we went to the front of the prison guard and the religious prisoners had gathered as well. We chanted the slogan of unity, struggle, and victory. Religious ones came up with chanting Nasro Menallah (help is from god). We could hear them as we were leaving the prison. Of course, the way they were chanting was threatening, and I will never forget the look of one of the religious prisoners. It was hateful and threatening. He later became one of the officials of the Shiraz Revolutionary Guards. Unfortunately, I have forgotten his name.

They brought prisoners from ward four, and we all gathered under eight. We did the usual stuff of freedom, and one of the prisoners of ward four gave me some books and said that they were my quota from the books in ward four, and since I was wearing only a shirt and the weather in December in Shiraz was cold, he also gave me a vest. He told me that maybe it would be a good cover until tomorrow that we could buy some clothes and said that the vest belonged to Mr Ghani Booloorian. And he gave me the books. (Those books in 1360 (1981), when the IRGC searched our house were taken by them, and as the mark of Adel Abad prison was on it, after insulting and obscenity, they destroyed them). We got ready to leave the prison, but after we were released, we had to go to the guard's office outside sign another form, and then we were released.

We went to the office of the Guard Officer, where Capt. Noshirvanpour was the Guard Officer that night, and he had a lot of respect for political prisoners. I had seen him in the prison since 1354(1975). He talked for a while and gave us the leave papers to sign and said we were free. The big prison door opened, and we were free.

It was about eight o'clock at night. I said that it would be about nine o'clock when we are released, and it was curfew at ten, and it was so dangerous, they might shoot at us. I asked them to stay in the prison that night. They answered they could not keep me. One of our friends said it was a conspiracy, what if they shoot us, who is responsible? We don't feel safe. The guard officer said according to law, they could not keep you any longer. One of the guards, who I had seen and known in prison for years, suggested I take them to the Setad square by my own car, and that they would have an hour and a half to go to a safe place by then. We all agreed to go with him, and he took us to the Setad square. After that, every single person was thinking for a place to stay for the night. We did the basic work of freedom and one of the children in ward four gave me books and said that it was my quota of the books ward four, and since I was wearing only a shirt and the weather in December in Shiraz was cold, I also wore a vest.

He told me that maybe it would be a good cover so that we could buy it tomorrow, and said that the jacket belonged to Mr. Ghani Bloorian. And he gave me the share of my book. (Those books in 1981, when the IRGC searched our house, took them all, and because the seal of Adel Abad prison was on it, and after a bit of insult and obscenity, they destroyed them). We set up and got ready to leave the prison, but after you were released from prison, you had to go to the guard's office outside the compound and sign another form, and then you were released.

Anyway, we went to the office of the Guard Officer, where Capt. Noshirvanpour was the Guard Officer that night, and he had a lot of respect for political prisoners. I had seen him in prison since 1954. He talked for a while and gave us the leave papers to sign and that you are free. After signing the leave form in The big prison opens and you are free. It was about 8 o'clock at night. I said that it would be about 9 o'clock until we were released from prison.. He said no, you are on leave and we can no longer keep you in prison. One of the children said that 10 o'clock is martial law and we will deal with martial law, and this seems like a conspiracy. If we are shot outside because of martial law, who will take responsibility for it? Will anyone be responsible for this massacre? We do not feel safe. Officer The guard said the sentence of release had come and you had to leave. One of the constables, whom I had seen and known in prison for years, suggested that I take them to the headquarters square by my own car, and that they would have an hour and a half to go to a safe place by then. We all agreed to go with that constable to the headquarters square and he took us to the headquarters square. After thanking everyone, he was thinking of a place for the night.

Of course, two of the children from Shiraz told us to go to their house, but those who were students said we would go to the dormitory, and in any case, everyone had a place to spend the night. It was only Maryam and I who had not yet chosen a place.

A personal Peikan stopped and asked for an address, and we showed him the way. We got in the car. The driver looked at me with that famous black prison slipper and the clothes I was wearing, and said sceptically, "Where are you going?" I said Zand crossroads. He said, "Do you have money"? I said yes. How much does it cost? He moved and looked at us in the car mirror with surprise. He was looking for an opportunity to ask us questions. Because this kind of cover was not acceptable in the cold of December and winter. Eventually his curiosity prevailed, and he asked, "Where do you come from?" The weather in Shiraz is cold in December, and you do not have proper coverage. I said that we had just been released from Adel Abad prison. He was surprised and and said, "Were you against the government?" I said yes! My cover is like this because I was arrested in the summer. He started talking about politics as usual and added that the government is spending its last day. He said, "Come to my house tonight and I will buy you clothes on the way." I said thank you very much .

We are going to find a hotel and tomorrow we have free time to buy clothes. He took us to the Zand crossroads and said that it was a good hotel.

I wanted to pay his fare when he said first of all I should say that it is free for you. Second, if you do not have hotel money, let me come with you and pay for your hotel. We thanked him and got out of the car. We walked to Dariush Street and the hotel, he introduced to us was a relatively chic hotel. We entered the hotel.

In the lobby, the hotel information manager was in a suit and tie standing behind the hotel counter, watching TV. I said hello to make him notice us. He looked at my clothes and appearance and said, "What do you want?" Some were sitting in the hotel's lobby watching TV. I said we needed a room for one night. He asked for an ID card and money. But not a birth certificate! He said that according to the law, he couldn't rent me a room without a birth certificate.

I told him that we had just been released from prison, and this was the prison phone number given to us by the guard officer, and that he could call there to make sure that we were a couple. After confirmation from the prison, he hung up the phone and shook our hand, saying he was glad to meet us.

At that moment, the national news started on TV, and he gave me the key to the room and left.

He gave me a long-sleeved shirt because it was cold. We went to the lobby, and they brought us tea. And following that, they ordered Kebab for us, and they started asking us questions about prison and its situation. It was interesting to them to talk with two political prisoners that had just been released from prison. We were answering their questions until late at night.

After that, we went to our room and for the first time in our lives, we were experiencing military curfew. The soldiers were armed in the street, and every now and then, we could hear them saying, stop! Stop! But there was no sound of gunfire. Luckily, our hotel room faced out the Dariush Street, and we could see soldiers on the street. In the morning, a breakfast tray was put behind our hotel room by hotel officials.

After having breakfast, we went to the lobby and told the manager that we would be back by afternoon, and we would settle the bill. We walked to the municipality and found a friend who worked with the municipality, and after greeting, I told him that we were in the hotel, and we had no money. And we needed money. I would pay him back later. He quickly gave me a lot of money and said I could pay him back after the revolution if we were still alive.

I happen to meet an old friend, Mohammad Ali Rahmani, on Dariush Street and we talked a lot, and we moved to the medical university and got a lot of information there, and we had lunch at the self-service. We decided to get tickets at four o'clock to go to Bushehr. No one in the family knew we were released yet. We also spent another night at the hotel, and in the first morning, I went to the Airport Square and bought two tickets to Bushehr at four o'clock and returned to the hotel. We decided first to settle the bill, and after having lunch at the self- service, go to Bushehr garage at Airport Square. After breakfast, we packed our stuff; we also had some pamphlets from various political parties, and we hid them in our stuff and went to the lobby to settle the bill and give back the shirt that they had given to us.

They said they were happy to host us during those two nights. And added the point that the hotel officials said that our stay was totally free and the shirt was a gift.

We were so happy, and we asked to talk and thank the hotel officials. He said he would inform them for sure, and we left and went to the medical university, which was not far from the hotel on foot.

After a lot of discussion, and meeting lots of our old prison friends and having lunch at the university self-service, we took a taxi to the Airport Square to move to Bushehr. We arrived in Bushehr in the evening. The family was excited about our release, and soon afterwards, almost all people in our neighbourhood were aware that we had been freed. Many people came to our house to congratulate our mother and expressed their joy and happiness due to our freedom. Of course, Maryam's family did not come. Because, during this time, SAVAK had put a lot of pressure on them. Even Some families who opposed me because of being against the Shah, came and met us. They asked questions like how did I get that time bomb and where did I want to put it? And how much I had been tortured in SAVAK and questions like this.

Until late at night, the locals came to see us and expressed their happiness that we had been released. The next day, some religious guys came to visit me, and they said asked why I did not have them come to greet me. I said that because the police are constantly harassing people and have killed some; so we preferred to come to Bushehr without having anyone know anything about it so that people would not get into trouble. Our house had become a place for left-wing supporters to gather over there.

As our house was close to the main street, it was a safe place for those who escaped from the police during the demonstrations. Many times, the guards who were violent and had been brought to Bushehr from Tehran to suppress people, attacked our house to arrest the protesters, but my mom would always help them to flee somehow, and we made a place and we hid some amount of gasoline and some glasses with to make Molotov cocktail with them, which came handy several times for the protestors.

They took Maryam's job as a teacher and transferred her to the exams department. Soon after, I started to gather a series of tools that we already had; we formed the Pishro Group.

I also went to the Hadish Company. It was the first time when I entered the office of Mr Vaziri, he stood in front of me as a sign of respect, and I was greeted by him; he asked the janitor to bring tea for me. When the janitor entered, I got up, and he came and kissed my face and greeted me with a laugh that I was no longer an employee, and he will bring tea himself. Ms Nobari also welcomed me and expressed her happiness that I had been released from prison. I took the opportunity and went to Mr Ghafouri, who said that he was going to Tehran to see Shukrollah. He had also been released.

Safaei was not around at all. I went to the company yard and met with several people I already knew or those who used to take part in fighting for illiteracy classes. Then I left the company. Without Mr Vaziri offering a job and Mr Falhvand had also left the company, I did not know the recruitment employee, and he was very happy to meet me and said he had heard about a lot about me.

We started replicating the pamphlets of the Fada'i Guerrilla Organization with the signature of the Pishro Group and tried to be active in the anti-Shah demonstrations. We tried many times to chant more radical slogans during demonstrations, but we didn't succeed. We kept distributing pamphlets. We would regularly meet prisoners who had been released from prison. Until one day, one of our friends said there was going to be a political meeting, and I should come too. Because political prisoners who have been released are supposed to go to the cemetery with a bouquet of flowers and read the resolution of the released political prisoners. That night, the meeting was held with several different views, and most of us agreed that Khomeini should not be mentioned in the resolution. We must try to defend the people of Iran in the resolution and condemn the massacre. In any case, hours later, a resolution was written that, fortunately, did not include Khomeini's name. Of course, that meeting only included men and Maryam, as a female political prisoner was not allowed to enter the meeting. Which, of course, we argued about it, which had no result. The offer to support the struggles of the Fada'i guerrillas was also rejected. And that then the struggles o f the people must be defended, and in any case the resolution was based on the support of the anti-dictatorship movement and the formation of a united movement against the dictatorship of the Shah and the demand for a democratic government. We all gathered as we had decided beforehand, in front of Ayatollah Hosseini's Mosque (Seyed Hashem Hoseini was born in the Bardkhun neighbourhood of Bushehr and was one of the Qom seminary teachers that considered himself as Khomeini's representative and was a trustworthy man among ordinary people). They brought some bouquets and a wreath around our necks, and we moved towards the cemetery in front of the crowd. The slogans were prearranged as usual and were played through their speakers. As we were advancing, they came and protested against Maryam's presence in front of the crowd, saying that she should go to the women's line. We emphasized that she should be with us among the political prisoners. But we faced protests from the organizers, and we agreed that she should go back to the women's line. When we arrived at the cemetery, the resolution was supposed to be read, but Mousavi Tabrizi was giving a speech that day, and when his speech was over, they dispersed the crowd and did not allow us to read the resolution and said now there is no time to read your resolution, and the crowd dispersed.

One of the guys chanted viva Marxist and Leninist ideas. Anyway, the crowd was dispersed, and we were not allowed to read the resolution.

We organized the Pishro Group and regularly reproduced the organization's proclamations and tried to spread them among the protesting crowd. I used to travel to Shiraz regularly and try to get more information about the form of struggle and to become aware of the latest analysis of the Organisation around the situation. I called our nomadic friends, and they said they were preparing weapons to use them in case it was necessary to attack strategic points in the villages and liberate them. I agreed with their idea. I also consulted our friends in Bushehr, who also had the same idea. We decided to gather more information about areas outside the city, specially mountainous areas to hide there in case of necessity, and attack the city afterwards.

It was decided that I had to go to Tehran in the hope of finding the friend of mine or other prisoners who had just been released from prison, and they were in touch with the Organisation directly. We went to Tehran University with one of my friends. In front of the university in the Book Bazaar, I got to meet many of prisoners I was in prison with. I got many books and papers from them, specially some by Abbas Jamshidi Roudbari that were great stuff. (Abbas Jamshidi Roudbari is one of the first people in the People's Fedai Guerrillas Organisation) and I got to meet Mahmoud Mahmudi there. We was so happy, and we hugged each other. He was with one of the famous political prisoners named Abbas. We walked together, and I explained everything to him, including talking about our new group, Pishro, he gave me his phone number to be in contact with him more. Meanwhile, he said that we must go to a safe house, which location had been leaked, to move all the stuff out of the home. That house belonged to a guerrilla whose name was Mahmoud, and he had been arrested there; we just moved all the stuff out.

I got to meet Javid Pashaei, who had already rented a house with some other released prisoners. I told him that I'd like to see the castle. He said it's closed; we can go to Jamshid Street, and we went together at night. What we saw there was a real disaster. (Qale' Shahreno was one of the neighbourhoods in Tehran, in this neighbourhood there were a lot of brothels an pubs. This neighbourhood was well-known with various names such as Jamshid, Ghajarha, and Gomrok. The most important of this neighbourhood was named Jamshid, which was set on fire before revolution in Bahman 1357 (February 1978) by Khomeini supporters and some innocent people lost their life during that event.)

I participated in some demonstrations with Javid in front of the university in the hope of finding a closer relationship with the Organisation. At night, we went to Nouri Riahi's house; his house had become a place for released political prisoners to gather. During demonstrations around Tehran University, most houses in those area would let demonstrators get in easily after fleeing from the guards; once Javid and I did the same and went to one of these houses after fleeing from police. The family welcomed us and even brought us tea, and when the situation was normal, we left the house.

Once we received a piece of news that we had to go to a hospital, they had put many books by Bijan Jozei at a point in the hospital beforehand. I quickly went there, and I found them. As I was leaving the hospital, a woman in a nursing gown came; she gave me some money and said this is help from me for printing the book. I thanked her and took the money and told Javid when I saw him and asked him to give the money to the Organization. He laughed and said that I should spend the money on my organization.

Anyway, we returned to Bushehr. With Mahmoudi's help, I placed the pamphlets, papers, and books in the car, and we moved to Bushehr. As SAVAK would sometimes search the cars that were entering the city, I got off in Borazjan and returned to Bushehr by a local minibus. In addition to distributing pamphlets, we tried to give a military form to the demonstrations by chanting radical slogans.

The first independent demonstration of left-wing parties was organized. We gathered in front of the Fanoos cinema and moved towards the Airport Square. We could mainly hear Tudeh party slogans, and we had our slogan as well; we would turn all around Iran to another Siahkal. The only way out was armed war. We overshadowed the slogans of the Tudeh party, which, of course, our slogans were mostly approved by young people. The people of Bushehr would curiously look at demonstrators who were chanting new slogans with raising hands that was usually a sign of left-wing parties' demonstrations. We reached the airport square, where the rest of the protesters were gathering. But they did not allow us to read our resolution and did not even allow us to approach the speaker.

26th Dey (on January 26), Bakhtiar received a vote of confidence from the National Assembly, and it was time for the Shah to flee Iran.

That day, again we gathered and tried to organise another independent demonstration of leftists with more radical slogans and emphasizing on the fact that Shah has fled from the country and overthrown of Pahlavi and in the slogan, we emphasised that the only way to be free was armed war. One day, we chanted in the form of war and escape and fled. I was alone, and I crossed the street to a place where several guards were standing, and they said stop! and I ran away. They started firing. I ran to my uncle's house and stayed in his house for a while. In general, we had infuriated the guards with our war and escape moves. Religious people wouldn't get involved themselves in these issues until they would make sure situation had calmed down, and after that, religious people and their leaders could be seen on the streets again. We reproduced the proclamation of the Organisation. Back then, I was in the Deir Port and after reproducing the proclamations, I picked some of them and participated in the demonstration of Deir, and after that, I distributed all of them, and then I ran away.

Later, once leftists of Deir told me that religious ones were looking for the person who had distributed those pamphlets and believe that they would kill that person in case of finding him because it also had a sickle and hammer logo. Despite all these problems we had with both the police and the religious people, we continued our fight.

Deir port is in the south of Bushehr province and is 208 km away from Bushehr and is one of the most important fishing and shrimp fishing centres in Iran and Deir is known as the largest fishing port in Iran. On the other hand, the religious people tried to remove our announcements from the wall to tear them. We would publish a multi-page bulletin called Pishro. We would put them next to the wall to let those who liked them to read them, but the religious ones would pick it up and tear it.

There was a man whose name was Namaki Vardiani, who couldn't read or write; the only thing that mattered to him was seeing God's name on the top of a page; otherwise, he would tear it apart. But whenever I was there around Shish Bahman neighbourhood, where most young people would usually gather; he wouldn't tear those papers. We had lots of problems with these types of people. One main problem was with Abdullahian Group.

Abdullahian were a group of religious ones who were waiting to find a chance to confront me.

The same group actually had most of the post-revolutionary physical clashes with forces other than their own. Their leader believed that a person named Abdullah would always come to his dreams and guide him. He was killed during the war, and they became the most violent organized forces of the IRGC and the intelligence of Bushehr. He had actually organised mobs and punks of Bushehr into a group.

They managed to organize all the mobs and idiots and gather them together in local committees to guard the night, and after the revolution, they became repressive and active forces of the regime.

On the morning of 12th Bahman 1357 (February1,1979), we were typing a proclamation in the house and also watching TV, which directly reported Khomeini's arrival, when one of our friends came and said that today the students who were protesting had been attacked and their demonstrations had been disrupted. Maryam was the organiser of this demonstration. But a few of the attackers who knew Maryam said she is a political prisoner and had just been released from prison. Neither beat nor insult her. We quickly went to the city; the demonstration was disrupted, and they had scattered all people.

We issued a statement on behalf of the Pishro Group and demanded that these divisive movements be prevented. Following that, we invited all political prisoners who had been released from prison to a meeting to find a solution to this problem. Of course, the Pishro proclamations were distributed, and each of them was torn to pieces by the religious ones. We knew that if we did not protest, they would suffocate us. And they do not let us breathe. At that meeting, it was decided to visit Ayatollah Hosseini, and we chose a representative to talk to Hosseini. We tried to attribute it to the divisive provocations of SAVAK.

Ayatollah Hosseini agreed for us to meet him. They explained that if we came to him, from the door we entered, we should sit and go to him. I and some of others said that we would not come, and it was decided that we would not enter the room; only the representative would talk to Ayatollah Hosseini.

As usual, only men were allowed to go, and they did not allow Maryam to come with us into the ayatollah's house and said that if she wanted, the women could make their own appointments independently. We were a group of prisoners who were got released from Shah Prison. We went to the Ayatollah's house. According to the previous agreement, the representative was allowed to go to Hosseini. And we all waited outside the Ayatollah's room. There was a large crowd in Ayatollah's house and several people started insulting and threatening. They were not happy that we were in the house of Ayatollah Hosseini, and they protested, and one of the villains became the head of culture after the revolution. There was a person named Ayatollah Taheri who was from Khorramabad, and he had also declared himself Khomeini's representative and was the main organizer of the demonstrations in the province. When he saw us in the house of Ayatollah Hosseini, he said sarcastically, "What do they want here?" Hosseini said that we were trying to stop these types of people, but they were out of our control. It was a spontaneous Islamic movement.

We did not understand Hosseini's words and left his house without any result. The only result was that these people want an Islamic government and we communists had to try not to provoke the Muslim youth. After returning from Ayatollah Hosseini's house, I met Maryam. I talked with her and told her that it's useless, don't go there, it just makes you angrier. Maryam said that she talked to some of our friends, and we have an appointment with Ayatollah Hosseini tomorrow. They returned from Hosseini's house without any success. We were afraid of the so-called local committees more than the Shah and SAVAK police.

Ayatollah Taheri had all the power and did his best to boycott us. Of course, we also had people who were popular among the people and were much more aware compared to them, but the reality was that mosques were under their control, and they could make people move whenever they wanted.

INITIATION OF ARMED OPERATIONS

We were approaching 19 Bahman (February 8), and we were trying to have a special program in memory of Siahkal on 19 Bahman. I went to Shiraz to meet some of our friends. Especially some nomads who would say that we were armed, and if the Bakhtiar government like the Shah wants to put more pressure on people, we'd use weapons. In Shiraz, the focus of the discussion was on 19th Bahman February 8), and that they had planned to invite Mahmoud Mahmoudi to give speech at the university, and they said if we had the opportunity in Bushehr to invite Sedigheh Serafat to Bushehr.

So we decided to invite Sedigheh Serafat to Bushehr, and we wrote slogans on the wall with Shirazis that night. I picked up some announcements with the organization's logo on them and returned to Bushehr. We had a meeting about how to write slogans. At night, the city was under control of so-called people's committees, who were now more dangerous compared to gendarmes and the Savakis.

We decided to wear Pouiani Hats, not to be recognised and continue writing slogans. (Pouiani hat was a special type of hat that only two eyes of the person were visible.)

We wrote slogans until late at night, and nothing bad happened. It was reported that the Organization has a program in Tehran on 19 Bahman. I went to get a ticket to go to Tehran, but unfortunately, I could not get a ticket, and I was planning to go to Tehran at all costs. In the morning, it was reported that they had attacked the police station. We quickly gathered and went to the city. Guards had fled, and the city was occupied by people.

We attacked the gendarmerie and got access to some weapons. One of the gendarmerie officers started shooting at us that was soon disarmed; a religious man whose name was Habib Zali announced with a loudspeaker among the crowed gathered in the city that the communists were getting armed and disarm them as soon as possible. They launched an operation very quickly and, first of all, disarmed one of us who had a machine gun, majority of people who had attacked the gendarmerie were known to those people. They disarmed everyone. Some were taken to court. Of course, I had a Pouiani Hat, but when I came to my mother's house in the evening, she said that they had searched the home before me reaching there.

This revolution started with shakedown of leftists' home and disarmament quickly began. One of the main reasons that led to executing Hamid Safarinezhad was having weapons; most weapons had been taken to his house after attacking gendarmerie and disappeared. Hezbollah was aware of that. We were constantly informed about the situation in Tehran through radio and television. Hosseini was a regular TV reporter, and it was during this period that Qassem Siadati, a member of the Guerrilla Organization, was killed in an attack on the radio.

We had found a Peikan to go to Tehran by that as soon as possible. We were five people, and we went towards Tehran. In Shiraz, we called some of our friends, and some others had plans to go to Tehran as well.

We arrived in Qom at night when some armed clerics stopped us, and I said that Maryam and I were among the released political prisoners and that they behaved respectfully towards us, and they marked the car glass by a marker. We arrived in Tehran without any problem. When we arrived, they stopped us and said that the situation in the city was dangerous and that they might shoot us. So it was better to spend the night there, and in the morning go to the city. We spent the night in a room that had caught fire due to the conflict and had traces of bullets on the walls.

Early in the morning, we moved to the University of Tehran. We reached the University of Tehran and the Fedai Headquarters. There was a large crowd in front of the headquarters. I called my acquaintances, Nouri Riahi, and he took us inside the headquarters!

All the old friends were gathered there. Over there, I met a friend who used to work in the Shiraz municipality who showed his membership card and that he was in the organization of the Tabriz headquarters and had just returned from Tabriz and was supposed to introduce me to the other people at the headquarters. They said that the headquarters should be evacuated. Meikdeh was captured by Fedai guerrillas. They rented a truck and moved the headquarters' equipment to Meikdeh in the morning until the famous meeting of the Organization on stadium turf of Tehran University.

I was constantly trying to get new information from the Organization. As soon as the meeting was finished, I took the resolution of the Organisation to Shiraz, and we used the facilities of Shiraz University of Geology and printed it, and we distributed them in the following morning in Shiraz, and after that, I took lots of them with myself to Bushehr.

When I arrived in Bushehr, they said that there was an exhibition at the girls' high school, which was supported by the Guerrillas Organisation. I went there and was surprised to see that the exhibition was a mixture of Tudehi and Fedai martyrs' photographs. I talked to the officials of the exhibition and explained that we have conflict with the Tudeh Party, and we will not stand together under any circumstances, and it was decided that they would collect photos of the Tudeh martyrs. At the same time, the Hezbollah members of the city came and started to shout and insult, and one of their leaders, Namaki Verdiani, came and said that I was different from the Tudeh members. And they had no problem with me, but they has a problem with the Tudeh members who are Soviet spies. I was just listening. I did not comment. I just explained that we will organize the exhibition tomorrow only with photos of the martyrs of Fedai. And the problem was somehow solved. And I talked to the exhibitors that said we had to be very careful. The situation was very sensitive, and we should collect the photos of the killed people of the Tudeh Party as soon as possible. Of course, this did not mean that we disrespected the victims of the Tudeh Party. The next day, the news came that during night they had attacked the exhibition and tore up all the photos of martyrs of the Tudeh Party.

Following that, the supporters of the Tudeh Party issued a statement stating that Fedai members and had mentioned my name and one of the other members. I went to the author of the proclamation and said that it was not right to mention the name;, we did not do that, and they did not accept it and spread the proclamation on a very large scale. We were supposed to answer them as well.

Anyway, I returned home angrily when I saw that Bahram Ghobadi and Azarnoosh Ebrahimi, Mehrnoosh's sister, were also at home. I was so happy that they were in Bushehr, specially the point that they had come to our house.

We talked a lot, and I told them the story of the Tudeh and that I was thinking of answering tothem. Bahram was supposed to help us in this work and prepare that announcement for us.

Ever since the news reached the fans of the organization that Bahram Ghobadi and Mehrnoosh's sister were in our house; our house was full of supporters of the Organization who met with their own eyes one of the first members of the People's Fedai guerrillas. We set an announcement to reproduce; it was reported that Mr. Alibaba had a poetry night in the Culture Hall. This was the best opportunity for us to read the proclamation while it was being distributed as well. We talked to Mr. Alibaba Chahi. He said that we can read aloud the proclamation during the night break and added that he was not a Fedaii, but I love the Fedaiis.

With the consent of Mr. Babachahi, we were supposed to read the proclamation aloud.

Among the students, a girl named Mehri was chosen to read the proclamation. The day, that we were waiting for it to arrive, and we went to the Farhang Hall. I could not believe the hall was full of people and one of the Tudeh fans came and said do not do this. I said then go and announce that the declaration was wrong, and we will not read our declaration. Some other members of Tudeh Party came to me and asked what weakens leftists' unity. I said we don't even accept you as leftists at all. Outside the hall, the debate between the supporters of the Organization and the Tudeh Party members and the miscellaneous people who had only come to listen Mr. Babachahi's reciting poetry, was fierce. Finally, we read our proclamation, and all those who were present at the meeting clapped for us. Our best achievement was attracting more students to our supporters. The Mujahedin Organization opened an office that was repeatedly attacked by Hezbollah. The Tudeh Party opened its office, which was closed shortly afterwards. We tried to do everything organizationally. We were specially successful in making a relationship with the workers of the Shahpour Company, which was the first ship production and repair company in Iran, and in the Oil Company we tried to stay in touch with the workers' council that had been formed recently. I was also supposed to go to Shahreza to solve issues around the accident, and I spent a night in a hotel in Shahreza, and in the morning, I introduced myself to the Attorney General; his surname was Kamali as well. After explaining the case that I was the one who had the accident and gave him my first and surname, he couldn't believe that I was telling the truth nor believing that I was giving him my real name until I showed him my Deprivation Card, which included my photo on it, then he believed me and continued that no official complaint exists about you. He continued that 13 people were injured during the accident, but as soon as they heard that you were against the government, they all agreed not make a complaint. Only the owner of the minibus has sued you and claimed damages. I asked the prosecutor to give me his address so that I could thank them. The prosecutor said that we were not allowed to give their address, but I would inform them that you have come here. The issue of minibus damage, we will refer its case to Bushehr. You have got no private plaintiff. After that, I moved to Abadeh and went to that restaurant and asked to meet with Samad. Of course, I explained the case to him.

And that point, I owed Samad 100 tomans. He said that Samad had travelled to Tehran, so I couldn't meet him. The owner of the restaurant did not accept the responsibility of 100 tomans and asked me to pay him if I could get to meet Samad in person. I went back to Bushehr.

The Guerrilla Organization proclaimed that we do not take part in the referendum on, 12th Farvardin 1358,(April 3, 1979).

Khodakhast, one of my friends, who had now a close relationship with the regime's repressive system, saw me in the city and invited me to get into his car and took me to the new SAVAK building, which was now in the hands of the Revolutionary Prosecutor's Office. They didn't release me until the end of the referendum. Afterwards, with the guarantee of Maryam, that gave them her Farhangi card (the card that shows you work in the educational system), I was released.

The Guerrillas Organization of the Abadan headquarters sent me a message to go to the headquarters of the Guerrillas Organization in Abadan. I reached the guerrilla headquarters in Abadan. I met Mahmoud Mahmoudi. We guarded all during the night, and over there, I also got to know Nasim Khaksar. Following the strike of unemployed diplomas in Abadan, we got in touch with them, and we took food for them from the headquarters. After some time staying at the Abadan headquarters, I returned to Shiraz with many pamphlets and announcements. In Shiraz, I gave a number of pamphlets and paper to our friends, and I left Shiraz and moved to Bushehr. An exhibition of books and publications of the Guerrillas Organization was organized in the Bushehr Farhang Hall, and in the afternoon, Hezbollah attacked there and set fire to all its books and pamphlets. During this attack, they also attacked one of the former political guys and wounded him with a knife. This movement was led by the Abdullahiun Group, whose headquarters were in the Sangi Turka.

An exhibition of photos and books by the Guerrillas Organization was held at the Bushehr girls' school. I was there as well, and one of the local Hezbollah members came and said, "Leave here because they plan to hit you on the head with a hammer and intend to kill you." I ran away from the back door of the high school with him. Hezbollah had gone and bothered a little and gone back and nothing significant happened.

Heidar Shanbezadeh played an important role in attacking there; he would always be informed through his father about things going on in the city, and afterwards, he would attack people based on those reports.

The strike of the unemployed diplomas of Bushehr started; they took refuge in the governor's office and all their meetings were held in our house, especially since I was passing on the experiences of the unemployed diplomas of Abadan to them. And how this strike should continue, and then they took refuge in the Bushehr governor's office, which was attacked by those carrying batons, and many of them were wounded and their gathering was dispersed. But then several them were employed in the educational system.

Once again, I returned to Tehran, and I was more comfortable there. Over there, I met Mahmoud, who was from Doroud. He used to guard in the headquarters; I also got to know his brother and sister-in-law whose name was Simin, and they were all political prisoners who had been released. Mahmoud's brother was named Ahmad, and he was a tailor, and in prison he was called the father. Meanwhile, I met a lot of released prisoners as well. I also got a lot of books and announcements and took them to Bushehr.

Cartons of books were put on the bus without me showing myself, but during this time, the theoretical differences between the Organization members were quite obvious.

After the moment, Ashraf Dehghani split away from the Organisation, and the conflicts inside the Organisation between members were evident. The leadership of the organization tried not to let these conflicts hurt the Organization. The focus of discussion reached the leadership level.

The Minister of, Mohammad Ali Najafi, started to fire many people. He fired many of the best and well-known s who were interested in the left-wing party. Maryam was also fired and, in fact, our source of income was cut off. Following that, my sister, who was a teacher, was fired. I had to find a job. Through the children of Shiraz, I was introduced to a metalworking workshop whose family was into the Mujahedin and Fedai Organisation. I started working in the metalworking workshop. We decided to take those who might be fired to the workshop and teach them metalworking so that if they were fired, they could work.

The massacre in Kurdistan, ordered by Khomeini, had affected the atmosphere of the city as well and nothing was normal. One night, when I was returning home from the city, local people were standing in front of the mosque. A member of Hezbollah named Abdolhossein Ardeshiri attacked me with a knife, and Mohammad Reza, one of my friends, rescued me from him. And he said do not come out too much or they will kill you. And I tried to communicate less on the street during nights.

SPLIT IN THE ORGANISATION, WAR AND START OF EXECUTIONS

The biggest split in the organization occurred in Khordad 1359 (June 1980); and the organization was divided into majority and minority. What happened had a terribly negative impact on the Organisation's fans who actually used to form the main part of the Organisation. Because until then, the organization had always tried not to let the conflict at the leadership level to get to the body of the organization.

I went back to Tehran and tried to obtain more information about the main roots of the split in the Organisation, which was not thoroughly clear to me. I had already obtained some informationfrom inside the Organisation at the leadership level.

They used to put a lot of pressure on me, especially on my mom. Hezbollah members would insult her every now and then, and they had boycotted her in our neighbourhood. Anti-communist and Fedai slogans were regularly written on the walls of the house. Through one of our neighbours who had given his house to Hezbollah, and they were monitoring our house.

My mother was told to tell her children to be careful as our house had turned to the base of IRGC members.

The day that Moscow Olympic opening ceremony was being held, which was around noon in a hot day of Bushehr, one of my friends who was a member of the Organisation as well was in our house that suddenly, the sound of a machine gun hit the quiet space of the house. My friend ordered us to lie on the floor, and I quickly got to the roof, but I did not see anyone because they had escaped on a motorcycle.

I went to the local grocer and asked if he had seen anyone, but he said he didn't see anybody. And all the windows in our house were broken. The next day, I went to the Islamic Revolutionary Tribunal of Bushehr and Maryam to the governor's office to file a so-called complaint. The Revolutionary Court said it was not related to us and referred me to the police station. At that time, Fatehi was the deputy governor of Bushehr. He was a reactionary and narrow-minded person. We knew each other thoroughly. He had told Maryam that I was killing them in Kurdistan! Our fellows will take revenge on you here. Anyway, I went to the local police station, and a policeman came and took a few bullet shells out of the wall and wrote down a report about what happened. Finally, he said they could do nothing, just take care of yourself, and the case of the armed attack on our house was closed without any care. We were threatened regularly in our neighbourhood, especially on those nights that they would chant Allahu Akbar. A 50cal machine gun was placed on the roof of Mohammad Davani's house, from that point they would fire air barrage at our house. We had cemented all the windows of our house, which faced outside to stay safe. We didn't have security. I was informed several times to be careful as they had some plans to attack our house with Molotov cocktails. We were mainly worried about Mom. I would rarely go home. If I was anywhere until late midnight, I wouldn't go back home. In fact, there was too much pressure on all political groups. There were frequent reports of clashes and beating our fellows; we all could feel a crisis was imminent.

One of the occasions that we organized was the anniversary of the death of Ali Akbar Jafari. I knew his sister; they used to live in Bushehr.

We planned, but we did not manage, to get a hall, and the anniversary was held at Rafiq's sister's house, which was welcomed by the fans, and we reported it to Rafiq's family with several photos. I was in their house for a few days. I took part in the famous 11th Ordibehesht demonstration, (1 May), which was the largest labour demonstration since the revolution.

Mahmoud took me to Kurdistan to see Kurdistan as well.

We held May 1, 1980 independently on the first of May. We formed a committee called the organizing committee on the first of May with the signature of the Pishro, and we got permission from the governor's office to march. Of course, we would guard every night until morning because we were repeatedly threatened by Hezbollah.

On May 1, we marched from there to the city when we were attacked by Hezbollah. The resolution was read out by a Shahpour worker who was himself a political prisoner, and we quickly dispersed the crowd before Hezbollah reacted violently. In this process, the Bushehr Painters Construction Syndicate actively cooperated with us. After that, we went to Abadan with a friend to become more familiar with the activities of the organization's fans. We could smell the smell of war. From there, we went to Tehran by train, which was my first experience travelling by train. I was so excited.

After returning from Tehran, once again, I started to work as a metalworker.

31th Shahrivar 1359(September 22, 1980). In the hot afternoon of Bushehr, the sound of several explosions came in a row, and we all ran out of the house in fear, and it was rumoured that the Air force and the Airport were hit. The war between Iraq and Iran began. I quickly went to guys in our neighbourhood and asked if there was anything I could help them. They said no. We built several trenches that some people came from Hezbollah and said that if we continued to build trenches, we would be suffocated in this trench; they continued that if we built these trenches to use against them in the right conditions, and we did not need them. Anyway, they tried to boycott us as much as possible, and at night, when Iraqi planes came and fired from the air, Mohammad Davani's friends also took the opportunity and fired air barrage at our house at as well. In fact, the beginning of the war was a good excuse for Hezbollah to attack us more. Those who worked in the Local Council often insulted my mother and said that we do not give products to communists. And sometimes, the old people would take Mother's coupon to the council and receive the goods.

On May 1, 1981, we arrived in Tehran with one of our friends and participated in the May Day rallies. The first time they left. And since we were in the house of his relatives, we managed to keep some of those who had escaped from Hezbollah in their house until morning, and they left the house early in the morning.

30th Khordad 1360, (June 20, 1981), I was in Bushehr. I went to Shiraz as I had heard about the mass arrest over there. The leaders of the Mujahedin had declared the beginning of armed struggle; soon afterwards, a period of repression, terror, torture, imprisonment, and execution began. Of course, the regime always had a plan to suppress. They were looking for an excuse to suppress all political parties against them. And June 20 was, in fact, the best chance for the regime to brutally suppress all political communities. Of course, the June 20 demonstrations were peaceful, and since the regime was looking for an excuse to show its dictatorship, they killed many people, followed by the mass executions of prisoners.

At that time, Saeed Soltanpour was one of the artists and members of the Minority Organization who was arrested on 27th Farvardin 1360,(April 17, 1981) on his wedding night and was executed on 31th Khordad, 1360, (June 20, 1981) along with Fazel and Saadati, mass executions began, and on 7th Tir,(July 28) when a large number of regime officials were killed in an explosion, our members who were already under a lot of pressure that even increased, and it became more difficult for us, who were known in the city as members of the Organisation, to live normally. One of the dead in that explosion was the representative of Bushehr; my friend had just gone to see what was going on because the representative was being buried at the airport, and Hezbollah had beaten him; he was hospitalized at home for several days.

I was working in the metalwork workshop, but I was aware of mass arrests and executions happening. Once again, I went to Tehran. I had been advised to be careful before moving to Tehran as almost all parts of the city were under control of IRGC and Committees. They were just looking for a reason to arrest anyone on the street.

I was in Tehran when I heard the news of the explosion in the Prime Minister's Office. 8th Shahrivar, 1360 (September 29, 1981). I went there with one of my friends to see what was going on. The city was not safe; when my friend found the situation dangerous, he said let's go home due to being afraid of getting arrested.

The situation in the city was very dangerous and some news of street arrests were widely reported. On 9th Ordibehesht, 1361(November 29, 1981), the news of the execution of Masha'allah Dastiyari and Mohammad Shatyari, as well as Hossein Andakhideh, a well-known teacher in the Bandar Deir, shocked everyone.

9th Ordibehesht, 1361(May 30, 1982), we became aware of Hamid Safarinejad's execution.

A few days later, I received the news of Maryam's arrest in Shiraz. The organization asked me to go meet her. She was arrested along with a friend of hers. Maryam was in prison for a while, and I used to visit her regularly. After a while, Maryam was released from prison. It was not long before we were both arrested in Bushehr. 1361(1982), Mosaiebi and Dadiari were the head of the Sharia Court; at the press office, an intensive interrogation ended with beatings and insulting, and both of us were taken to the Revolutionary Court in the house of Mohammadian to receive a final arrest warrant, and afterwards, we both were transferred to Helali Prison. Maryam was taken to the women's ward, and I was taken to the men's ward.

My interrogator was a man from Abphakhsh neighbourhood who I had met him several times previously when I was staying in the veterinary dormitory of Tehran University. I think back then he was student of veterinary. After going through the legal process, I was transferred to the ward. The Helali prison had a big hall and all wards' doors faced out to that hall. There were also two solitary confinements, which were located behind the ward two and ward four. Right in front of the head of the prison's room, there was another room that was used for interrogation.

The prison was full of prisoners from various political parties, and the Tavvabs (a group of prisoners who had become the regime's supporters under the prison pressure) still were not so powerful in the prison. Hefazi was the head of the prison, and his deputy was Hasan Gharibi. Alidad Bahadar was one of the most famous interrogators who was violent, and his main task was interrogating members of the Mujahedin Organisation.

Gholam Keshtkar was the interrogator of leftists who had an active cooperation himself with leftists until before joining the IRGC; of course, nobody would consider him as a betrayer as he was not that smart or aware of the whole situation that existed in the country. He was from a village and as he had a lot of information about fans of the Organisation, IRGC had employed him. The prison was mainly full of the Organisation's fans. It was noon, and it was time for the prisoners to rest and sleep; as a result, I was waiting in hall four until 4 p.m. that the cells' doors would be opened. I knew almost all prisoners who were from Bushehr. I was transferred to ward two; over there, I knew almost all of them. Gradually, some signs were revealed in some of the prisoners to become Tavvabs (a group of prisoners, who had changed their ideology and became the regime's supporters due to being under pressure in the prison), some of the prisoners were moved to Shiraz and Karaj, who became violent Tavvabs. When I was in prison that was a chance for me to get in touch with prisoners from various groups with various ideologies. I would discuss with many of them and that was really useful to get to a good conclusion.

My mother had gone to the Revolutionary Court many times but couldn't get permission to visit me. Tashakori was the Revolutionary Court investigator at that time. Once my mother said that we were standing in front of the court with several prisoners' families when he came and my mother had gone to him and asked about us situation, but he had insulted my mom. My mother became angry and said that he were worse than Savakis. He answered back and said he was Savaki. My mother said that I used to visit my son at SAVAK period for many times, but you are worse than them. Tashakori continues his way and says nothing and enters the Revolutionary Court. We were released. It was later revealed that this type of arrest was common throughout Iran and was only to identify people and have new photos of them. The fans of the Organisation held a photo exhibition and invited me to go there. I went there, and soon afterwards, one of the people in our neighbourhood came and said, "Run away. Yusufu, the uncle of Gholam Keshtkar, is planning to kill you". Javad had not yet finished saying that some Hezbollah members were getting close to us from distance and were chanting. Majid was passing by in an Aryan car. I took the opportunity and fled. My mother had heard about that day beforehand that they were going to kill us, so she had gone to the exhibition with my little brother, and they had beaten my little brother and broken his camera. My mother had saved him from Hezbollah members.

One night in those years, I was writing a slogan with Qasim-Gh when they found out, and we escaped, but several bullets were fired at us, which fortunately, didn't hit us. The city was no longer safe. So I decided to go to Shiraz from Bushehr. In the meantime, I opened a metalworking workshop with my mother's money and some savings, and with the participation of a relative. Our partner took the opportunity to try to steal our money, and I went to the police to complain that they had made the workshop to a Teami Home (a home which was used for political purposes). Of course, the police didn't care, but after a lot of difficulties, we were able to get back some of the money from this man and his son. This was a sign that Bushehr was no longer a safe place to live. I told my mother that Maryam has left the city, and was leaving too; and I suggested that she sells the house and come to Shiraz. I got an address in Shiraz from a metalworker I knew so that I could find a job in Shiraz. Of course, this metalworker had two brothers who were members of the Mujahedin who had fled abroad, and I was forced to go to Shiraz.

My mother's situation was very difficult in the neighbourhood. Because whenever she would go out, she was insulted in some way. Those who used to insult her during Shah period and would say that her child is a saboteur and would speak in favor of the Shah, were now Hezbollah and considered us infidels and dirty, and this time, they put more pressure on my mother, especially with the excuse that we were filthy according to Islam. After being forced into exile with my father a long time ago to Lar, once again, she had to send herself into exile, but this time to Shiraz. I went to Shiraz, and I found a job in a metalwork workshop. Of course, I did not have any information about Maryam's situation. For a while, I lived with an Abadani family who were supporters of the organization. The situation in Shiraz was not okay, either. I would just go straight from home to work and came back trying not to get close to the city center. I lived in my aunt's house for a while so that I could find a room, and during this time, I managed to become a member of a metalworker and mechanic in Fars Province.

During this time, I became one of the activists of that union. We tried to visit the workshops that the metalworkers didn't have insurance and provide them with one so that they could join the union. And several times, I was about to be beaten by their employer. Because I had a car license, one of my duties at the syndicate was to buy from the Ta'avoni (a union that serves in favour of a particular types of workers in each field) for metalworkers and mechanics Ta'avoni. The syndicate had turned to a place for leftist gatherings. During this period, a housing Ta'avoni was formed, which was supposed to take a plot of land for eligible members from the urban land. During this time, the Shiraz Workers' House began to put pressure to control the union. A secret war broke out between the mechanic metalworker's union and the workers 'house, and the workers' house tried to break up the union. I managed to find a new job in a metalworking workshop in Fakhrabad and started working. They were very good people and that their brother was arrested after returning from India and was imprisoned in Evin for a long time. They had very humane treatment towards everyone.

Maryam also called me during this time, and we got in touch. Of course, after a short time, Maryam said it was better to get divorced. In those circumstances, I was shocked and asked the reason. She only said that we no longer have anything in common, even politically so. So it was better to get divorced amicably.

After days of arguing, I accepted and decided to find an office and get divorced. Of course, I knew an office where the mullah had been forced not wear his special clothes anymore, but he had the office, so it was easy for us to go to that office and separate. We went to that office together, and one of the old friends who had the radio and television repair, was also a witness, and we got divorced.

The Organisation had cut almost all its connections. The only way was a bullet in which served as a way for members to find each other.

There were some organizational activists in the syndicate, and I approached them. I was looking for a room at that time because it was difficult to live in my aunt's house or sometimes in the workshop.

Anyway, I was also looking for a warehouse because my mother was selling the house, and we needed a warehouse to store the furniture they bring from Bushehr so that we could buy a house. A house was found in the neighbourhood of my aunt, which was for a woman named Effat. She had migrated to Shiraz during the war and had separated from her husband. It had an extra room that I could rent and stay in until I bought a house. After talking with Ms Effat, we rented a room and a large warehouse in the house. The house was safe. I would sleep there at night and waited for my mother to come to Shiraz. During this time, an emotional connection was formed between us, and this emotional relationship led to a friendship.

I explained my situation that I was in prison, and I did not have a clear situation at the moment, and Ms Effat also liked me, so we got married. Needless to say, she also had a son from her ex-husband. I was not in contact with the members of the Organization that much, so I had not told them about getting married. My mother also moved to Shiraz, and we managed to find a two-story house in the Gol Koob area of Shiraz. We all moved into that house, and we rented the lower floor to one of the fans of the Organization. Of course, I would meet Mary from time to time and informed her about getting married again. She was trying to leave the country and even Majid said that he would take her to Dubai for free, but she didn't accept. She got a fake passport, and through one of our relatives, we were aware of the date she was going to leave the country.

One of our friends said that her passport was suspicious, and she shouldn't travel by that. She didn't care, and the day she was supposed to leave Ira, she and her brother, who was in the airport, were arrested.

I was informed that afternoon by the same acquaintance that she had been arrested at the airport. We informed the organization.

The house we lived in was not safe anymore; especially since one day a piece of paper fell into the house, which said if we agreed to cooperate, put a sign on the electric pole next to the house that I shared that with a friend of mine, and he said that it was suspicious and seemed that the house was being controlled by police. We asked that friend to vacate the house because the house was mortgaged by the bank, and we had to pay the bank monthly, and it was a bit difficult. Mother sold the house and bought houses near an aunt. I also rented a house on the Airport Road, the address of which I had not given to anyone, and I had a single room at the gate of Kazerun, which I sometimes would go there as well. Effat was pregnant, which I had to deal with logically considering the difficult security and economic conditions. Until Shahrivar 1363 (September 1974), when my daughter was born, I went to the hospital with one of my friends by his Peikan car and brought her home. Due to the difficult conditions, I could not give an address to anyone, but my friends would help me. The issue of the child's name was another problem. I went to the registry office and asked for a birth certificate for my daughter, and I chose the name Lena, which was opposed by the registry office. I chose Mehrnoosh, in memory of Mehrnoosh Ebrahimi, a People's Fedai guerrilla who was killed in 1950 by SAVAK. Mahmoud Namazi, who took me to the hospital by car, was later arrested and tortured to death in Qazvin. He was one of the Guerrillas' Organisation members. I told my daughter all these stories when she grew up.

RETURN TO HOMETOWN, ARREST, AND TORTURE

The life in Shiraz had become difficult. The members were willing to be connected with Bushehr. I vacated my house and the room, and I found a career in Borazjan and moved there. We found a big house there that a part of that had also been rented by another member of the Organisation who had come to Borajzan mandatorily as well. I stayed there for some time until one of my friends said that he would go back to Shiraz, and he went there. So, I found another room in another house and started living there. The landlord's son was also one of the Organisation's fans who was kept in Bushehr's prison, and I knew him. I had met him while I was in Bushehr's prison. During this time, they arrested one of our members in Shiraz. One of our friends' sister's and his father were arrested in the airport as well while they were carrying a report of our Fars and south meeting in a book. That was when we found out that our calls had been controlled while we were talking with people abroad.

At the airport, the intelligence service had directly opened that particular book and accessed the reports. They were taken to Tohid prison to be interrogated. And after interrogation, they were both moved to Evin prison alongside two other prisoners who were wounded. They were looking to find our friend who was sister, and his father had been arrested. I took the responsibility to hide this person.

We went to Borazjan together, and he lived in the same room secretly with us in Borazjan for a while until we managed to find another place to hide him, and I sent him there. And I became the liaison between this friend and the Organization, which I had to perform once a week with the liaison of the organization in Shiraz, and I informed them of his situation and his health. And I passed on his reports to them. Another problem was about his family had guessed that I was the one having information about him, so they tried to get in touch with me. They had found my mom's house in Shiraz, and they had sent a message, asking to meet me, which was not logical due to the situation. I rented a room in Shiraz to easily get in touch with Jamshid. Jamshid had a green minibus, and we would hold all our meetings inside, considering all points not to get caught.

Our friend was in a safe place, and we would go to him regularly and report to others that he was in a healthy situation. My lifestyle had made life so difficult for Effat, specially considering the fact that I was not a good economic situation as well, and I would spend all my time for political activities, and I had no more time for my personal life. Of course, she was right. I had also made a connection with Bushehr, and we had made a group and tried to find some particular addresses to send the bulletins to them. We were so busy, which was not favourable for Effat, who loved to live a calm life. I owed an apology to all three of them.

The situation between us got so bad, having lots of quarrels and discussions up until a point we decided to get divorced.

We separated, and she moved to his previous house in Shiraz with her two children. I also moved from that house to another room and transferred that friend from this secret place to this room. And I used to meet regularly with the members in Shiraz. One day, I went to Shiraz, and they asked me to hand over my friend to them. I handed him over to Shiraz while considering all the security issues. I found a job in Saadabad. Saadabad is 24 km away from Borazjan and 80 km away from Bushehr port.

And from there, I managed to stay in touch with Bushehr, but I didn't give my address to anybody, and most of them thought that I was living in Shiraz.

Jamshid said that we should be more careful because of the situation on the 19th of Bahman, and he made an appointment that was in Isfahan but said if we couldn't find each other, go to Isfahan and make an appointment there. After 22th Bahman, again we met each other and since then we would meet each other once a week in that green minibus. One afternoon when we saw each other, I noticed that a yellow Peikan was following us, and he parked the minibus, and we went to a restaurant. We checked the outside of the restaurant, and we made sure that the yellow Peikan was following us. I had two reports with me. I eliminated them in the toilet, and I went back to the restaurant hall. We were sure we were under control.

I sat in the restaurant, and Jamshid left the restaurant alone. After paying, I walked to my mother's house, where I made sure that they were not following me anymore. After making sure that Jamshid was not arrested, I returned to Saadabad.

During this time, I was suffering from a chronic sore throat, and sometimes, I was coughing up blood. I thought I had tuberculosis. I went to Saadabad Clinic, and the doctor there told me t o see a doctor who was an ENT specialist. I went to Shiraz and visited an ENT doctor who was also into the Organisation. He said that I had a Laryngeal polyp, and I had to undergo a surgery. I explained my situation to him that I had no money. He said he would fix everything to perform the surgery in Morsalin Hospital, which was under authority of IRGC, and he told me after having the surgery, I needed to leave there as soon as possible, which I accepted. I had a meeting with Jasem, and he gave me an address to go there in case of not being able to hold my regular meetings anymore. My nest meeting was with Jamshid in a room; meanwhile, I was sure that I was being controlled. I went back to Saadabad. Over there, I would work as a metalworker, and I had made connection with three members of the Organisation, and we were supposed to meet each other regularly. I was also in touch with Bushehr. I would go to Borazjan to a private place that I had chosen beforehand. I would bury all the papers, and after getting s report from my friend, he would go there and pick those publications and pamphlets. And we would set another meeting as well. Once again, I went back to Shiraz, and we held a meeting with Parviz. He explained that they were in touch with abroad, and through these channels, they could get access to publications and pamphlets. I would usually meet Parviz on the street. We would walk together, and he showed that he had cyanide under his tongue and that we would mostly meet while having cyanide under our tongue. I went back to Saadabad. At our next meeting, Jamshid said the situation is too dangerous and asked me to pack my stuff and move to Shiraz. The pursuits had increased significantly. Most people would feel they were being chased. I went to Saadabad, packed my things, and returned to

Shiraz and went to that single room. My illness was getting worse day by day. I needed to have a surgery as soon as possible. Once again, I went to the doctor and explained my situation. He said he would fix a time but don't forget to leave the hospital as soon as possible after having the surgery. There was a barbershop that I would use as a means to tell other members that I was in an okay situation without the owner of that shop knowing anything. I mean I would go there and talk with him for a while, and after that, my friend would be informed by that owner that my friend was there and asked me to say hello to on behalf of him.

I went to my mother's house and spent the night there. I called the doctor's office, and he said if I was ready, go to the hospital. I said I was ready, and my sister and I went to Morsalin Hospital on Khayyam Street in Shiraz, and the doctor came and told me to change my clothes and be ready and go to the operating room as soon as he signaled. I also waited for the doctor, who gave me signal at about eleven o'clock in the morning, and I passed by the nurses, who did not say anything because they saw the hospital clothes, and secondly, they saw that the doctor said it was my time. I entered the operating room anyway. It was time for the doctors to rest, and the operating room floor was full of blood. The doctor and one of his assistants came to help the doctor for free.

The operation was done only with local anaesthesia. Part of my laryngeal polyps were operated, and the doctor gave me an ointment and a pack of pills from his pocket and told me to leave the hospital immediately, and me and my sister took a taxi home, and I rested at home for a few days.

After that, once again I went to that barbershop to let others know that I was okay. Once again, I got in touch with Jamshid and told him about the surgery I had. Jamshid told me that the situation was very bad, and also added if I could, leave the country. I went back to the room that I used to live in.

But every time I made an appointment, I realized that I was being chased. I tried to ditch them as much as possible. Of course, I told this to Jamshid, and added that if the next appointment was not made, there was an alley that he was supposed to go there and go to a grocery store. I also asked him to draw a line on the electric pole with marker, and I was supposed to add another line to it until it turned to be a crossed so that we could understand that it was safe to meet there. This meeting was also cancelled. At night, I went to the room, and tomorrow in the morning, once again, I went to meet him, but again, I couldn't. I vacated my room. I went to one of my friends' workshops, and he accepted me to work there and to stay there at nights, which was good for me. The only problem was with the owener of the workshop who was addicted to drugs and that was why the police would check him every now and then. I slept there some nights, but I did not feel safe. I left some stuff there with my friend's permission, but I had to sleep there so spent some days standing that situation without having anywhere to go at night. One night, as I was walking at the Moshir crossroads, hoping that I might see one of my old friends, a person touched my shoulder, and I was shocked. He was a friend of the workshop owner. He asked me to go to his house, and I said no.

I was not well. If I was arrested and put under pressure, I might give them the address of your home, and I don't want this to happen, and I do not want anyone to get in trouble. He said, "Come in, I live in Jale square. Let's go". I went to the house of that friend who was very kind, and his wife was from Jahrom and his brother was a close friend of Saeed Soltanpour and said he used to work in Abbas Agha theatre.

I stayed there for a short time, and I wouldn't go out that much as I was afraid of getting arrested. I went to street again. And I tried to meet one of the Organisation's members. I decided to go to Isfahan, which we had talked about earlier if it was necessary. I went to my mom's house. My nephew was our guest, and we talked and joked until late. Then I took a shower and packed my things in a military bag to leave in the morning. Early in the morning, the doorbell rang. My nephew opened the door, and I could hear him saying he I was not there, and another person told him to have me to call. I quickly set fire to several reports in the bathroom that I had with me. I opened the paper, which included the meeting location in Isfahan. I tried to memorise it and set it on fire as well. My nephew closed the door and said uncle had come from the gas department and said that I had applied for a job at the gas department. But believe me, they were guards. I quickly packed my stuff, and I went to the roof and through a few rooftops. I got to my aunt's house. The mother also put on clothes and came to my aunt's house.

With my mother's help, I went to the main street, got on a taxi, and engraved my mother's anxious face in my mind for the last time. It was not long before I saw the same yellow Peikan was following the taxi very slowly and cautiously. I had nothing special with me. The taxi arrived, and we all got off. I got on the first minibus toward the city centre. Because in the centre of the city, I knew a lot of different places I could easily ditch them and then go to the garage and get to Isfahan.

I had a bag that was like the bag of those who had just returned from the war and did not draw any attention. I decided to go to Fakhrabad, the workshop where I used to work and stay there for some days, this way I could get a ticket to Isfahan afterwards.

I went to there, and H was there as well. We talked for a while. I asked him to buy me a ticket to Isfahan. He said I looked so anxious.

"Anything wrong"? he asked. I said not really. I drank a glass of tea. He said he needed to call one of his friends, and after that, he would buy me a ticket.

I was sitting in the office, and I could see the outside. Suddenly, a white Peikan passed in front of the office, and for a moment, I felt bad from the light of his gaze. I said I do not want a ticket and left. He asked if I became upset. I said no, I just have to go, and I went out of the office and moved to the gate of Kazerun to go to the garage when I saw the white Peikan was parked, and I went back to escape. Two people got out of the Peikan and attacked me before I could escape. They beat me, and two other people were found, and there were four people, and they shouted that I was an addict and smuggler, and they kept beating me.

The workers all came out the workshop and were looking at this scene. When they were beating me, I looked at H and how he was looking at me. They arrested me and pushed me inside the Peikan and started beating me and asking for my name and my address. I refused to answer. They threw a blanket over m y head and continued beating me. One searched my pocket. After a short distance, we arrived at the intelligence headquarters, which was behind the former regime court. Its big door opened, and we went in. They forced me to get out of the car in front of a small door. There was a steep slope. We passed that slope, and afterwards, they pushed me into a small room.

In the car before we all get out, I was blindfolded, but I knew that area very well as I had come to visit Maryam there. We entered a small room.

An officer was sitting there. They stripped me naked, but they did not take off my shorts and inspected my whole body. And he wrote my name in a notebook and with my eyes closed, he took me to a corridor and a guard came with the hose in his hand and said take the hose and come. I followed the guard with the hose in my hand. The corridor was actually where I had visited Maryam several times, but we were outside the corridor meeting the prisoners behind a small window. For a few moments, I was left behind in a waiting room. The sound of crying and moaning filled the environment. After a few moments, the room opened, and I was pushed into the room. There were about four or five people there. They asked questions; the sounds were different. I was led to a chair, and one of the interrogators asked for the name and address of the house. I gave the address of my mother's house and my name; they knew me. But they were looking for another home address that I did not have.

One of the interrogators said that I wouldn't leave there alive. They asked me to give them organizational information and who I was going to meet. I told them I don't work for anybody, and you have got me wrong. They continued beating me, and they kept asking me to tell them everything that I knew.

I felt that my face was swollen, and the fists that had hit my side and abdomen made me nauseous. The room became empty. There was only one person in the room, and he asked very slowly, "Do you know Jamshid?" I said no! This is the first time I heard his name. They kicked me, and I fell on the ground with a chair. I was unconscious for a moment. He lifted me off the floor and told me to sit on a chair. And he asked, "Do you know Jamshid?" I said no! There was another voice saying something, but it was too slow for me to understand. Once I felt he was hitting me on the head with slippers, which was very painful. Then everyone left the room, and I was alone. The tactic of interrogation is to put pressure on you and then give you a chance, and that attack actually creates fear first and then gives you a chance to think.

After a long time, the door was opened once again, and some people entered the room. One called my name and said all your friends have confessed, and you don't have anything to hide. He punched me in the face, which made me dizzy. One said to get up, and I got up and took my hand to the corridor and asked me to sit next to the same door. He said I should not talk to anyone. Not to raise my blindfold or I would be beaten. And went. Then a guard came who had slippers on and asked very slowly, "Have you eaten anything"? I said no, I should go to toilet. He said nothing and left. He brought me some bread and cold stew. Again, I said I need to go to the toilet. He said not to talk, just eat. I started to eat until they called me once again. I went to the same room.

A few people came and told me to sit down. I sat on a chair. A voice behind me said not to look behind me.

"Well, don't these items seem familiar to you"? That was familiar! I said no, and he said "Don't you know him"? I said no! He started beating me, and I definitely said that I do not know him. One of them said that we have received a ta'zir sentence for you (the ta'zir sentence means the sentence of flogging to death). He continued that he did not want to beat me because everything has become clear; I had nothing to be beaten for because of that, they even followed me to Saadabad, but I went from there. "Where were you"? he asked.

They showed me some pictures of Jamshid, including the one in which he was in the minibus; I said I didn't know him. They punched me again, and they took me back to the corridor.

They were trying to scare me. There were some people in the corridor who, like me, were waiting for interrogation.

It was an opportunity for me to think about what information to give so that the interrogator would give me information, and I would be less likely to be beaten. In any case, now was the time to use my experience. No one came to me anymore. In the evening, a guard came and asked my name and left. After a while, he told me to get up and follow him, and he took me to the ward. I went to a solitary cell where two other people were. I went into the cell, and after greeting, sat at a corner.

I knew one of them; first, I thought that maybe I had met him in the metal and mechanic syndicate, but I didn't remember quite complete. He seemed to know me as well.

He introduced himself and added that he was arrested due to being related to Rah-e Kargar, and the next person introduced himself and added that he was arrested in Abadeh and was related to the Fars organization and was a relative of the representative of the majority Organization, and he was from Abadeh as well. He said that he had been beaten a lot in Abadeh. Of course, based on my experiences, I said believe me, I do not know why I am here and why I was arrested. I added that they said my accusation is related to the Majority, but I think they made a mistake. But Muhammad somehow signalled me not to say anything. I slept after dinner, and after breakfast, they called both of us for interrogation. We waited for the guard to come and take us to the interrogation room. We both sat behind the same door, and we were not allowed to talk with each other.

The interrogator came and took me to the room. He said we are allowed to send me to the prison and added not to do anything to go downstairs and be beaten. They gave me a chance to think. Now say whatever I have and relax my mind. I said, believe me, ask whatever you want, and I will tell you. He said no more. "You write, not us asking." He showed me a photo that Jamshid and I were in the green minibus together, and I was sitting in the front as usual, and it was clear that it was me. He said I knew everything, and this was my photo. He said they had all the information. "Say everything and do not bother yourself". I said he was travelling, and I was a passenger of a minibus, then they punched and kicked me a few times. He said I must go downstairs, and we went down. After two or three steps, I was blindfolded. We got there; I could barely see that it was a small room, and I saw a bed in the corner of the room.

He called one the guards whose name was Abdullah (over there, they would call each other by this fake name, Abdullah, while whipping). He came to me and said to lay on the bed. I went to bed and slept, and they tied my hands on both sides and tied my legs together and put an old, dirty blanket on my face. I had experienced whipping before, and I was ready for it. The first whip to the sole of my foot could not be explained at all. I tried not to shout, but I couldn't. I do not know how many times they beat me when my first shout was heard. After a while, the interrogator came to me and said that they would stop if I started to tell them everything to be recorded. They started once again; I shouted I would tell them whatever they wanted. I started to explain to them my relationship with Jamshid, but I just to a specific extent. The interrogator seemed satisfied, and they opened my legs. Back then, the worst part about whipping was when they would stop, and instead, they would rub something on my feet that would made the pain worse. They opened my hands, and the interrogator said if I didn't say all the things, we would go downstairs again. This time, we wouldn't stop anymore. I started to write, and I mainly focused on writing about fighting against Shah and supporting the people's fights against Shah. The interrogator came to me once again and tore all the papers apart. He said I'd like to beaten; it's clear. He went out, entered the room after few moments, and said write everything! If not, they would take me downstairs again. I was afraid of going there once again, so I started to write. I wrote about the Syndicate and things we did there. He didn't like those things either. He took me downstairs once again, laid me on the bed, tied my hands, and threw a blanket on my face and started the tape recorder and said end to the whipping is highly dependant on how much I talk, and they record. After few whips, he called Abdullah again and said I needed to be treated more professionally. He added that I was sick. He told me there was like a hospital, and their main duty was to provide treatment for sick people.

After whipping for a while, Abdullah left the room. The tape recorder was still on. They both left. After few minutes, the interrogator came back and asked if I recorded anything. He was speaking slowly as if I felt there was also another person in the room, and he didn't want me to understand that. I said he could ask me anything, and I would answer.

He said he would give me another chance. "What was your relationship with Maryam about"?

"What did you have to do with the Organization? Who were you going to introduce to the Organization? How many times has the military official of the Organization (he meant Anoush Lotfi) come to your house in Bushehr"? The questions were horrible. "What information do you have about the members of the Air Force"?

Of course, I was in contact with some members of the Air Force and had introduced them to the Organization. I was in contact with them until 1361 (1981). We were just friends. And I'm currently in touch with two of them via Facebook. I ignored the fact that a person named Lotfi came to our house and denied that I was acquainted with the members of the Air Force. And I said that Maryam had her personal life in both her private life and job. They opened me, and we went upstairs. Again, they asked me to write down everything, and they left the rom. They didn't ask any other questions about Maryam and the Air Force. I wrote down all the things I knew about the syndicacte. After a while, a person came in and took the papers and led me to the cell where Mohammad and that worker were.

But this time, I was wounded. That night, I asked for my toothbrush and toothpaste, and they brought my toothbrush to me. A person came and asked if anybody needed any bondage. I said I did, and they bandaged my feet.

In the morning, after having breakfast, they called me once again.

Mohammad and I were taken next to the interrogation room. After a while, they took me to the interrogation room. The interrogator said to open my blindfold; don't look around. He showed me some pictures and asked if I knew them. I had seen some of them in the past, but I firmly said no! And just when I saw Jamshid's picture, I said I knew him. The interrogator said we have got all information from you, so I didn't need to repeat useless information. Again, they repeated their words and said write down whatever I knew about Maryam. I said we used to live together for years, but when it came to the Organisational life and activities around it, she used to work very secretively, and I had no information about her life. Especially because we had learned not to be curious. Again, he asked me some questions about Jamshid and our relationship and wanted to know some information about the syndicate, but he didn't ask me anything about that member of the Organisation who I kept for such a long time. I was so happy that at least I had not given any information about that stuff to them. It seemed like they had no information about that stuff, or at least it, was not important to them.

At night, Mohammad and I were taken to another cell. Another man was in the cell as well. He welcomed us. His face was so familiar to me. He introduced himself; he said he was a chemistry engineer who had been graduated from Shiraz University and had been arrested because of the Mujahedin Organisation, and he added that he had been in that cell for one year by then. We talked with each other a lot about ward four and those years in prison. Mohammad was wondering why I was only talking as a person just related to Syndicate, nothing more. Unfortunately, I have forgotten that man's name.

Tomorrow, once again, they called us to be interrogated. Mohammad went in, and I stayed outdoors. A person came and said to go, and he took me to a hall that included some Arj chairs, which were mainly used for exam days in universities. He said we had a lot of time, but he was not in the mood for talking a lot! He said write down whatever I knew. He gave me some paper and left. The handle of the chair was full of slogans. Be strong, death to the traitor, viva different political groups. Again, I wrote down the things I had written yesterday. I ate lunch and in the evening; a person came to me and took me to cell but this time alone. They didn't read the papers while I was there. I spent the night alone, which was a good chance for me to think about everything carefully and get ready for the upcoming days.

The following morning, the cell door opened, and they took me blindfolded to the toilet. After coming back, he asked if I was ready for praying. I said I don't pray. After having breakfast, they took me to the interrogator room again. The interrogator threw the papers angrily at me and asked what the items were. "Do you want to write a book? We have heard a lot about these stories. Go and write again." This meant to me that it was end of the interrogation, and they were not going to beat me anymore; again, I went to the same hall and started to write.

In the evening, a guard came and said keep this hose and follow me. In the corridor, there were some prisoners who were all blindfolded. They were all standing in a line, and the line started to move. The first person was a guy from Kazerun. They took a picture of us, and once again, we came back to the corridor. They divided prisoners into groups. They took me to a cell that was managed by a guy from Kazerun and had been arrested because of Mujahedin as well. He opened my blindfold and asked what I had done. I said they got me wrong. He became angry pushed me to the wall and said here nobody is supposed to lie. And he started to threaten me, and after few moments, he said that's my room; do you pray? I said no. He said "Really"? I said, yeah, I don't pray. He asked why. I said I don't. He called a person, and they tied two yellow straps to my slippers, as they didn't want anybody else to use those slippers as they believed I was filthy.

He led me to my room and gave me two blankets, a piece of plastic that was a tablecloth, a plastic cup, spoon, and a plate that belonged to me, and they added that it should not be mixed with their equipment. There were only two Jews living in that room, so we were three people and two separate tables; they said that I was not allowed to touch anything, and they specified the toilet that I could use, and I had to follow all the rules and regulations. At that moment, I saw a friend going to the bathroom. Ali, who was a child of Abadan and was a good photographer. He saw me and pretended like he did not know me at all, so I did not tell him anything, and I started a difficult life there. The sound of Salawat kept coming everyday, and the smell of gallop pervaded the whole ward, and I can still smell it.

I sat at a corner and after having lunch. I wanted to go to the toilet, which they didn't allow me to do, so they said I had to go to toilet after them because they believed that we were dirty as people who didn't pray.

It was night when everyone gathered in the corridor. I saw the two Jews crouching in the corner of the room, looking at them in horror.

I sat in the same corner of the room they had given me and watched them. The voice of Salawat, followed by a person, was praying and the sound of crying was heard. Following that, they started to chant slogans like death to infidel, death to Monafegh(hypocrites), which was terrifying, and I felt that each of us might be attacked until the prayer was finally over. Someone came and said you we were not allowed to go to the bathroom until the brothers' work is over. Then we could go to the bathroom. I said yes! Someone slapped me and said, "Didn't they say you are forbidden to talk? Why did you talk"? The atmosphere in the ward was terrible. They would count prisoners at night, and everyone should have said, Abdullah! Fortunately, it did not include the three of us in that room. Prayer nights were horrible nights.

A few days passed, but with the fear that any of them might attack us. The two Jews also refused to come to dinner with me. Because, after all, they believed in God, and they considered me as an atheist. One morning, the person in charge of the ward, who was from Kazerun, came and said that I should shave my mustache and pray. I said that I have not reached this conclusion yet. He looked angrily and left, but since then, I felt some prisoners were trying to make me angry or at least tried to scare me. As they were passing in front of my room, they would look at me angrily.

I was completely boycotted. Similar to Adel Abad ward one in 1357(1979), when most of the demonstrators were religious. The prisoners of the ward were divided into two groups, clean ones and dirty ones, as I was not religious like them. But fortunately, I could at least exercise individually. The worst situation was when they would pray; typically, they prayed three times a day. I was just afraid that they would attack and beat me.

One day, they called me. I went out with a blindfold on. They took me to the interrogation room, and as I entered, a person slapped my face and asked what I had written down. He continued that I was supposed to write down the reality. Again, they asked me to write. I could remember what I had written previously, so once again, I wrote all the stuff down, but this time, in another way. In the evening, they took me to another cell, and they had taken my stuff there beforehand.

For sure, living in solitary confinement was way better than living in that terrible ward. One day, around noon, a guard came and said get to ready and pack my stuff. They took me out of the interrogation area with a blindfold on. And I went to the small room, which I went there in the first place when they brought me here. They gave me my stuff, and two young men came to me and handcuffed me, took my hand, and led me out of the prison. Outside, after getting on a Peykan, I was handcuffed to the car door.

A young guard was sitting next to me and told me to close my eyes and show me a Kalashnikov under the blanket and said not to think of running away at all. They had the right to shoot. The car started moving, but before the car started moving, they told me to lower my head, and I also lowered my head with my blindfold. As we passed the Third Army Square, I noticed that it was heading towards the Airport Square. I told myself that they were taking me to Bushehr, which was bad news for me. Because Bushehr meant taking revenge on me. When we passed the Shiraz Road police station, they opened the blindfold, and I saw the faces of three people. Shortly after, they changed way and went on a dirt road. I was terrified that if they went to Bushehr, why did they change the way to the dirt road. They threw a blanket over me. They took a short dirt road, and the car stopped, and three people got out. I could only hear them opening and closing the doors. After a while, they removed the blanket from my head and opened the handcuffs and told me to get out. I got out, and they handcuffed me again.

I stood at a corner wondering what they were going to do; they talked slowly with each other. They said to get in the car and handcuffed me to the door.

We returned to the main road and moved towards Bushehr. I was no longer blindfolded. In one of the cities on the way, they went to the gendarmerie, where all three went to the toilet. They said if I wanted, I could also go to the toilet, and I went. We didn't eat anything on the way. We arrived in Bushehr. Again, I had to put the blindfold on. I felt like they had lost the way and didn't know where to go, and by mistake, we went to the governor's mansion, which was the center of Bushehr's intelligence service. It had some cells as well and some of the mass executions of 1360(1982) had taken place there.

After talking with their authorities for a while, they came and said that they would not take their responsibility and added that we need to go to Helali Prison, and we entered the terrible Helali Prison. I was handed over to the office of Helali Prison, head of the prison, Rasool Ranjbar, used to live in our neighbourhood, and I believed that he was one of the two motorcyclists who shot at our house. I entered the boss's office. I was in a bad situation as my feet were bandaged, and I couldn't walk easily. I had not bathed for several days with a long beard and long hair. He looked at me contemptuously and said, "Finally, you are here!

We were waiting for you. We had received some news of your arrest, buddy!" They opened my handcuffs and, of course, they said goodbye to me and left for Shiraz, and I was alone with Rasool Ranjbar and the dreadful prison of Shokri or Helali!

I was sitting in the room when several guys from the city came, all of whom knew me. They came, looked at me, and left. Rasool Ranjbar said that this was the end of the way. I wouldn't get out alive. He spoke from the position of power and added that they had destroyed all other groups; his words reminded me of when I was arrested for the first time in 1353(1974), that the head of SAVAK in Bushehr treated me the same. He handed me to a short guard who knew me because I was in prison before. And we moved to the ward. He led me to the cells of ward one. As I explained, Helali Prison had two solitary confinement cells behind the public ward, Wards one and four. Each had eight cells. He led me to the cell and closed the door, and the guard explained that I could use the toilet three times and not to speak loudly and close the door.

The cell length was eight steps and four fingers, and its width was three toes and four fingers, so I could not even sleep properly. It was summer, and the cell air was unbearable. I was sitting with the door opened. I did not stand. He was one of the local guards whose name was Kargariani, and I knew him. Suddenly, he kicked me hard and said when he entered, I had to stand and insulted me and communists. I stood, and while I was standing, he again punched me several times and then left. Bushehr was set for taking revenge of me. I knew that, and I had to be so careful not to give them any excuse. I had fled from their traps several times. Finally, I had been caught by those who had shot at our house, and this time, they were determined to kill me in the prison.

About two o'clock in the morning, my kidneys began to ache. At that, he limited and closed the environment and the fact that I could not get any medicine. The excruciating pain of my kidney was about to kill me. After a lot of screaming and moaning from kidney pain, finally, a guard whose name was Zendebudi came and started to insult me and left. I was barely conscious as I had a lot of pain until morning.

In the morning, they brought breakfast and a painkiller, but the pain did not go away. They took me to the interrogation room while I was still suffering from my kidney pain. Hamid Gholami, also known as Hamid Arab, was an Iraqi immigrant who had joined the Revolutionary Guards after the revolution and was currently serving as a prison guard and was considered as the prison torturer. I went to the interrogator's room, and Hamid Arab stood in a corner. The interrogator said from the moment that I was connected to them, they were informed and they went to Saadabad to find mr, but I had left; otherwise, I would have been arrested sooner. "Now take this notebook and pen and write whatever you know. Here is not Shiraz! This is Bushehr and you have to say everything". I was badly suffering from kidney pain, and he asked if I was in pain. I said yes since last night. He ordered Hamid Arab to give me another pain killer. and he continued that they had a lot to do me; they needed me alive. He said to write down whatever I knew about Maryam. And then he opened his Samsung bag and took out a pistol and said no one knows you were arrested. If you want to bother me, I will kill you with this gun. So think about it and say whatever we want. That's all we want from you. I went back to the cell with some painkillers.

The pain went away soon. As I was tortured during the arrest, and I had shouted a lot, which was near to my laryngeal surgery, it had a bad effect on the vocal cords, and I could not speak properly, and at the same time, it affected my breathing. I informed the prison authorities several times in various ways that I was not feeling well and that I had surgery recently and needed a doctor, but they did not care at all.

Another important issue was taking shower. It had been about a month and a half since I had taken a bath, and I smelled bad. The only time that I could barely wash myself when I was allowed to go to the toilet. Finally, after many discussions, they agreed to go to the bathroom at noon, but since the water was coming from the water source and the source was on the roof, it was boiling water; despite all difficulties, I took a bath. The next issue was eating dinner, when the cell was completely dark and I had to take a bite with one hand and with the other hand determine the path of the bite to the mouth, which was very difficult. I would eat with a spoon. I took the spoon with my right hand and would guide myself with my left hand to my mouth. In general, I was hungry most of the time. After many discussions, they agreed that I could buy a can of figs from the store. Of course, they deducted the cost from the money I had with me when I was arrested. I rationed the figs, which was a big help. At the same time, the empty can of figs helped me to urinate. Which was great as I only could go to the toilet three times a day not any more; after emptying the can, I would take it to the cell again, which was not favourable for prison guards, so I was also confronted with protests and corporal punishment by the Revolutionary Guards. The interrogator's tactic is always to put you in solitary confinement and cut off all your communication, and your only communication is with the interrogator. Sometimes, you might get tired of seeing him, considering that the result was insult and torture, but at least for a moment, you can get rid of being alone; and if you were not experienced, you would consider the interrogator as the only sign of hope left for you. That was the tactic of all the interrogators. I also began to recall the books that I had read by then and exercised regularly, and I knew a little about mathematics that I could put into use. I would always try to exercise as much as possible to get tired and fall asleep easily at nights.

With the pen and a 200-page notebook that they had given to me, I made a tic-tac-toe to play with and tried to keep my mind active; After a while, one day the interrogator came, and I asked him to let me go into the exercise yard to breath in some fresh air. After a few days, they let me do so at one o'clock in the afternoon. It also had a story of its own; at one o'clock in the afternoon in the hot weather of Bushehr, which was terrible, I asked them to let me take a shower, and the interrogator made fun of me and added I was not in a hotel. One day in the morning after having breakfast, Hamid Arab came and asked me to pack my stuff, and added that I would be sent to Shiraz!

Hamid Arab took my hand and led me to the office of Rasool Ranjbar. In the office of the head of the prison, they returned my bag and the money they had taken from me during my arrest, and the head of the prison said that I was going to be transferred to Shiraz! We went with Hamid Arab to a minibus and, as usual, he said I would be killed if I tried run away, and like these repeated words that many times I had heard. But in the minibus, there were only Hamid Arab and me and the driver.

The head of the prison escorted us with a patrol and a companion. In the minibus, I learned that I was being transferred to Shiraz, and from there several prisoners were being returned from Shiraz to Bushehr. After 1357(1979) that I got released from the prison, it was the first time that I was going to Adel Abad prison once again. As usual, they got my clothes and wrote every detail. I knew some of the guards, and they welcomed me; a plain clothed man took me to ward four. I knew ward four thoroughly, but the new ward four was totally different with the one I was being kept there before revolution. A thin guard who was singing Arabic songs and talking to his friend was preparing to go to the battlefield. As I was waiting there, I was reviewing my memories of the day that I was taken here first. Back then, I was full of passion; not so today. I had heard a lot about Tavabin and terrible things that they had done. After few minutes, the guard came and asked my name and other details.

He introduced me to room seven. The man in charge of the room was a Tavvabi Mujahed whose name was Behzad and was a pharmacy student at Shiraz University and originally from Kermanshah.

He explained the rules of the room and said I was not allowed to talk to anybody except him. He continued if there was a problem, go to him. I went to room seven, which was next to the staircase. He suggested the middle bed and asked if I prayed; I said no. He said it was the wrong place for me. He asked me not to touch anything until he was back and then he left the room. I didn't know anybody in that cell; I just sat at a corner and waited for Behzad to come back. After a while, he came back. I was in that room for around an hour until they called me and asked me to pack my stuff. Then again, another guard came and asked my name and other things. After a while some plain clothed men came to me, among them, there was a man on wheelchair who was disabled thoroughly from the waist down. Later, I heard that he had been attacked by members of the People's Fedai Organisation. He asked me if I had been transferred from Bushehr. I said yes. I have just come from Bushehr. He asked me if I pray. I said no. He asked if I would cooperate, I said no. He continued to ask what I meant by saying what do you mean by saying cooperation? He said take him to Andarzgah.

Andarzgah was a newly-built ward next to ward one, and it was somehow a place for keeping those who they wanted to put them under pressure.

Ward one was for women now. They asked me to wait. I was trying to find out more about this newly-built ward until a guard came, and to my surprise, they took me to ward four once again and led me to the same room, room seven.

WHY DON'T YOU PRAY BEFORE STARTING TO EAT?

B ehzad came to me once again and asked, "Don't you really pray"?
I stuck to the same answer. He said, "I suggest that you pray
to have a better life". I saw that all prisoners would pray in the
ward, so I said okay, no problem. I would pray as well, but I just tried
to act like them nothing more. The first issue was meal's prayer. When
they would set the table and everyone was sitting around, they recited
a prayer called the table prayer. I did not pray. I was asked to go to the
second floor, known as the Assessment Room, that day. The second
floor in front of the room was completely covered, and I stood outside
the room when the curtain was pulled back, and they called me into
the room. There was no bed there, and they had spread blankets around
the room. They told me to sit down. I sat on the floor.

They gave me a clerical table and some blank papers. The first
question was why I do not pray at the table. I asked to explain. I explained
that I had an acute laryngeal problem and could not speak loudly, and
this effected my speech as well. So now I stutter. Because of this, I could
not recite the prayer of the table aloud, and he noticed that I was shouting
to let them hear me. He said I could talk in the room now but were not
allowed to talk in the ward, which was a good point. And asked if I had
anything to say. I asked what he meant. He asked if I had given all my
information. I said that I had been interrogated in Shiraz and Bushehr
and had given them all the information I had.

He said if I had nothing to say, I could say it now until it's not too
late for that, and he let me to go back to my room. I told Behzad that
I had gotten permission to talk with other people in the room as well.
Behzad asked if I had ever been to ward four before? I said yes, around
two and half years in addition to another six months. He said be careful
to obey Tavabs' rules, not to be punished; for instance, before revolution

while serving our prison sentence we had got used to brush our teeth while standing in line before going to toilet or taking shower, which was against their rules.

Strict conditions were applied in ward four by Tavabs, which had made it so difficult to live there. We were not allowed to even act in anyway that we wanted to while having food or even washing our face; we had to be so careful. Once the interrogator asked me if I wanted him to send me to the public ward to have fun. I didn't understand what he meant back then, but

later, I heard something about there in ward four. They didn't bother me because of having moustache. I went to the second floor, the bank of the prison; I deposit some money that I had, and they gave me a depositor's book to let the family members deposit to this bank account if they wanted to. On the other hand, we were not allowed to get any fruit or other stuff from those who would come to visit. They could deposit money on that bank account, and we could buy our stuff through that. Taking showers had its own specific rules and each room had a specific hour for taking shower. Before the revolution, the story was totally different, and we could take shower whenever we wanted. I got to meet Khosro Moeini accidentally in the ward. But still, I was not allowed to talk with anybody, so I couldn't talk with him, and also one day, I met Naser Mahani and Abou Taleb Nezhad in the exercise yard, who without letting others see him talking with me, gave me some information about the prison that was so helpful for me to get used to the prison's situation.

We had a specific daily prison schedule, we had to wake up at 5 a.m., and after saying prayers, we had one hour to rest, and after that, we would go to breakfast, and after that, we had various classes until 11 a.m. From 11- 12 a.m., we couldrest and do personal things that we had to do. After that, we said prayers, and after that, lunch, and after lunch until 4 p.m., we had time to rest, and later, class until evening praying. We had dinner, and again, we had time to rest, and at 10 p.m., it was lights-out.

Classes were on different days, and they were all compulsory and listening to special Friday' speeches was mandatory as well. Taking part in Quran' class was compulsory as well, and some other classes were voluntary. One day, they asked me to go to the assessment room. Several people were sitting on ground cloth, and they invited me to sit on the floor, and the interrogation started and they said I did not give information; they started arguing and putting a lot of pressure on me with insulting but without physical torture, and once again, they banned me from talking with others. I was only allowed to talk with Behzad, and I had to start my plan considering the fact that I was not allowed to talk with anybody. One day when I was talking in the exercise yard, a person came to me and started to talk with me. He was one of the Mujahedins and had become Tavab. He focused on Islamic dialectics and economics, and I was a good listener. Of course, the mission was from the second floor, which was the Tavabs' Publishing Centre. They worked there from morning till night. Back then, it was said that their leader was a man from Jahrom, who oversaw the Peikar Organizing in Fars Province. All prison programs and classes were organized by the same room, and from time to time, they brought a movie that we had to watch. One of the problems in the room was that if you would sleep on your front, they would wake you and make you sleep on your back as they believed that in that position you might fart, which was considered as disrespecting god. Some of the Tavabs would go for guarding at nights in the city and would sleep in mornings; those people were so strong in the prison.

I was waiting for court, and it was famous that you would be taken to the helicopter room. All prisoners would be gathered in the waiting room of the court. There was no difference between addicted people or political prisoners who had to be tried in a revolutionary court, and it had a fan that would make a terrible noise, so that room was well known as helicopter room.

Every now and then, they would give a form to everyone and ask everyone to fill in the form, and it was mandatory. They would ask for full details and the name of the organization and the organizational category and the level of education and opinion about the Islamic Republic. Ward four was full of Tavabs; they were everywhere. I had not any visit yet, and I was not able to inform my family where I was. I also had trouble breathing due to a problem in my larynx! At the same time, I was stuttering while talking, and I had to shout so that the other person would notice me talking, and I asked to go to the hospital several times, but the prison authorities did not care at all, and from night to morning in the room because I could not breathe properly, I was also a problem for my roommates. One day, I was taken to a prison clinic and a doctor examined me and said that a specialist doctor should examine me. The doctor said he would write a letter, and I left there with a few painkillers.

I spent the whole winter in ward four. One day, they asked me to go to the office. I knew some of the guards; one of them told me I can not even compare old political prisoners with the political prisoners today as they were trustworthy, but these new ones are even worse than guards, and they are not trustworthy at all, and they quickly report everything. They were talking with each other, not me, but I could hear them. After the legal processes, I was handcuffed and taken out of the prison door by bus. Several prisoners with various crimes were accompanying us, and they unloaded them on the way, and the policeman opened my handcuffs and said, "Do not escape." I said, "No, I did not do anything to escape." We walked to the clinic and waited for the doctor.

After a while, Dr. Rishi came and examined me. He knew that I had come from prison. He asked me why I was imprisoned, and I explained that I had been arrested by mistake.

After the examination, he said that it was not important and continued that I should be careful, and I knew all those explanations myself, and the point that I should not talk too much, speak loudly, and it would get better in time. I came out of the clinic with the police and waited for the prison bus. My hands were opened, and we were talking with each other outside of the clinic. The guard was making complaints about prisoners' behaviour, and he said these new prisoners even report about other prisoners as well. The prison bus came, and we got on and went to the prison, and I went back to ward four. The life in the prison was just as always. This disease had become a reason not to let Tavabs annoy me that much (The policy of making Tavabs was implemented in the prisons of the Islamic regime in the sixties, and during the process, frustrated political prisoners would turn to Tavabs by interrogators and prison officials.)

Despite their remorse and disgust for their past struggles, these prisoners were kept in prison, and their existence was used to advance the government's goals in various fields. Tavabs in the prison actively suppressed other political prisoners and cooperated with prisoners and prosecutors. Tavabs were used in street patrols with the Revolutionary Guards to hunt down fighters outside the prison. This would increase the atmosphere of terror in the prison, break the atmosphere of struggle in the prison, and the prisoners' distrust of each other.)

Once again, I was asked to go to the second floor, which was managed under the authority of intelligence office in cooperation with Tavabs.

They told me they had seen some sortsof paradoxes in my behaviour, and I had to be interrogated once more. They said go think, and they would call me back again. This time, their behaviour was threatening, and deep inside, I was thinking to myself that they might attack me. All of them were Tavabs of ward four. I went back to room seven, and I continued my tough life there. One day, they said pack your clothes you are supposed to be transferred soon. I packed my stuff and got ready to move. Two other people were with me; when the legal process was over, they put us in a car that looked like an ambulance, blindfolded us, and we left the prison. My guess was that we were going to the IRGC Information Center behind the former regime court, which was the IRGC's secret and dreaded prison.

We went through its small, scary door, and they started to search us in that famous little room, and with the equipment we had brought with us from prison, we sat in the hallway in front of one of the interrogation rooms. After a while, someone came and very slowly asked everyone's details. We were all facing the wall and blindfolded. After asking the details of each person, we were taken to a place. I was also sent to a public ward. There were about 25 to 30 people in the room, and the person in charge of the ward came and handed me over and asked me about my name, details, and organizational affiliation. I said, I am a member of the union of metalworkers and mechanics.

They gave me two military blankets and a pillow, and they also determined where I had to sleep. At night, everyone stood to pray, and then the food prayer was said, and after that we had dinner. There was a terrifying atmosphere. All of them would pray. One of the members of the Mujahedin, who was from Ahvaz, had lost his mental balance and was constantly cursing, was taken out, beaten, and returned. He made himself dirty, which caused problems for all the prisoners, and one night, some of Tavabs took him to the bathroom and beat him severely, and then handed him over to the guards outside. I tried to keep myself busy with the small library that was there so that no one would come to me. Anyone who asked me a question, I would answer that I was working with a trade union, and I started reading Motahari books for a while.

We were all young, and I was considered as one of the old guys there at age 28. One day, after having breakfast, they took Jamshid to the ward. I was surprised and happy to see him after a long time. In the exercise yard, we would usually walk together. He had been tortured a lot. All his face was wounded and after flogging his foot soles, they had also flogged his waist.

We talked a lot, but never got into a discussion about getting arrested and the cause. During this time, we could not attract a large number of fans. After a few days, they took him out of the ward. The interrogator called me; I went to the interrogator's room. The question was what discussion did we have with each other, and I said that he did not just talk about his organization, just normal discussions.

Jamshid other members of the Mujahedin were supposed to be executed. Of course, he told me himself; after talking with the interrogator he had been returned to the ward as they wanted to show their power. One afternoon, they called me to the visiting room. I was blindfolded and went out. The interrogator was waiting for me outside and said, "Do not talk about the prison and things going on here, otherwise, the meeting will end, and you will be taken to the basement". We went to visiting room in an open area. They had built several cabins that were protected by bars and barbed wire, and a net was drawn between the visitors. A person was standing behind me who I could not see his face, and the visitor couldn't see him at all as well. He would control our conversations. We were not allowed to turn back to see his face. Ten minutes of meeting with my mother after that long time was so enjoyable to me, she said that my sister had gone to Kuwait and did not know about my arrest; the man behind me didn't notice to this part of my mom's talk and was not important to him. Mother said if they let her, she would come to visit again. She was crying in all those ten minutes; after my release, Mother explained that during this period, Adel Abad prison officials had told her that they did not know where I was. The committee, the press, had told her that they were not aware of my situation. In Bushehr, she had been told that I had not been arrested at all. After a long time, she had found me through an acquaintance who was familiar with the Revolutionary Guards.

I was called again for fingerprints and photos. I went and was returned to the ward; no one would talk about their crime case with anyone, Tavabs were in power there, and fortunately, they wouldn't argue that much over there. One day, around two o'clock in the afternoon, they asked me to pack my belongings. I got ready to get out of the prison, and the guard came and went through the same steps and I got out of the prison. I was blindfolded and taken out.

Three people were waiting for me. As usual, they said if I ran away, I would be killed. I had heard these words over and over. We moved from Shiraz to Bushehr without stopping, and I was handed over to Bushehr prison in the evening. After being handed over from the Shiraz Revolutionary Guards, I was transferred to solitary confinement in Ward four, which was located behind the women's prison. My cell was at the end of the ward, and it was completely dark. According to the solitary confinement rule, it was like ward one. But this time, Hamid Gholami, well-known as Hamid Arab, was the main solitary guard of ward four. It was completely closed in the cell and had only one window, which the guard would open from time to time to look inside and check the prisoner. Bushehr summer had begun. It was as if I had to spend the winter in Shiraz prison and the summer in Bushehr prison. All those previous guards were still working there, the only difference was that in ward four, two people from Borazjan were guarding, and in general, they were not violent towards prisoners. Just one of them whose name was Gharibi would bother prisoners time to time so badly, but compared to Hamid Arab, they were good guards.

Since I was transferred from Shiraz prison to Bushehr, all my belongings were in Adel Abad prison in Shiraz. I had few items in Bushehr and a small amount of money. Because all my money was in Adel Abad Prison Bank, I needed money to buy some food, and I shared it with the prison officials who said that if the guards went to Shiraz, they would tell them to bring it to me. But after a while, fortunately, my mother came to visit me, and I received some money.

The month of Ramadan came, and I announced that I could not fast because I was ill, and I did not face any bad behaviour from the prison authorities.

On the other hand, I was in solitary confinement, so I didn't need to pray as well. Once again, I planned, and in that small cell, I started, and I followed the plans. The weather was hot, and I would walk in the cell with only underpants on; once Hamid Gholami opened the window and saw me with underpants on. He started to punch me and asked why I was walking like that and told me I shouldn't wear clothes like that again. I had problems for going to shower and exercise yard as well, as they didn't let me.

I felt that I couldn't control myself mentally. My sleep was disturbed, and I started talking to myself. Yet I tried to control my psyche by recalling the books I had read and playing math and sports. In addition to that, the pressure of the prisoners led me to lose my self awareness. Once I asked the guard who was Borazjani to give me shaving materials if possible because I was in a terrible condition. He came after a while and said to get ready to go to the shower. He added that he had also brought shaving materials. I was very happy. I thought that if I had a chance, I would eat those stuff and kill myself because I had lost my temper. It was the best opportunity! We went to the bathroom with the Borazjani guard. He poured the ingredients into a bowl and opened the door and said use that quickly and give back the bowl. Actually, they were experienced enough not to give the stuff directly to me so I couldn't commit suicide.

I waited for a while and then I started taking shower when he shouted from outside that it was over. Unfortunately, some of the materials were not cleaned, and I just tried to clean them with my shirt and my body burned badly. In any case, I managed to visit Rasoul Ranjbar, the head of the prison, and he agreed to give me a cream from the prison clinic to treat me. This was welcomed because I was running out of patience and could not do anything. In the mornings, the interrogator would sometimes summon me to discuss politics. Of course, he was the speaker, and I was the listener. Day by day, my physical strength was decreasing, and I was losing my mental balance.

Once when I was in a really bad situation, I started to hit the door with a punch and acted aggressively until the moment that Akbaripour, the guard of that day who was not a violent guy, showed up and took me out to breathe in some fresh air. That was a great help for me in that situation. Once or twice, I felt very badly, and they came and gave me water and let me sit in the corridor outside the cell.

There was a Borazjani guard who sometimes would leave the door of my cell open when he was guarding, for hours, as long as I wouldn't go outside.

One day when I made a lot of noise, Hamid Arab, he was the guard that day, came and slapped and kicked me a few times and told me to put on my blindfold and took my hand and drag me to a warehouse outside the prison, which was like a barn. There was a lot of straw on the ground. He handcuffed my feet and tied me to a point that was attached to the wall, and I could walk within a certain limit. I had lost my mental wellness completely; this was exactly what they were aiming for.

Hamid Arab threw me in a room that was like a barn and left. He went and said if I became hungry, straw was enough.

I shouted a lot; my voice could no longer be heard. A few days passed. One day, the small door opened and one of the prison guards came and ordered me not to get up. He said if I got up, a terrible punishment would be waiting. It was not long before my mother entered the room. She was scared, seeing me with a long beard and hair, and the room that room smelled very bad. After I was released, my mother explained that when she saw me, she was terrified, and thought it was not me for one moment, and I thought that they had brought me there only to harass me. "This was not you. You were sitting on straw. With a long, messy beard and hair. When I came to hug you, a guard stopped me, and you shouted that you do not want to visit me anymore". Mom continued that when she left the prison, she walked the streets like a crazy person and cried wondering what they were doing to me.

After visiting her, they took me to the ward once again. This time to a cell in ward four, which had a window facing out the exercise yard. This cell was way better than previous ones, cells in ward one and four were about 115cm * 170 cm, but this cell was about 2m * 2m, which was easier for me to exercise there and also walk. They took my stuff from the barn, which I had been kept there for a while, to this cell. I asked them to take shower as I was afraid of getting lice. Again, the Borazjani guard took me to the shower, considering what happened last time in the shower, I quickly washed my hair; afterwards, I washed my entire body. This time, it was great, and that Borazjani guard who I can't remember his name, gave me more time to freely take shower.

TAVABS IN THE PRISON

From the moment I entered that cell, the voice of Tavabs could be easily heard, as they would surround a prisoner every day in the yard and would force them to repent by insulting and physically assaulting him. Terrible sounds of calling someone with things such as evil, evil, execution must be done, death to infidels, could be heard all day in the yard. Sometimes their voices could be heard from the prison hall as well, which was terrifying. Nevertheless, it was clear that there were still prisoners resisting. In any case, this cell was much better than the previous cells, and the window that opened to the yard was effective on a person's spirit, which helped me a little bit mentally to get better, but hearing Tavabs' shouts itself was a form of torture for me, and I was thinking all the time what would happen if I was taken to the public ward?

All nights they would all pray in the yard, and after that, punish those prisoners who Tavabs believed needed to be punished. The interrogator was proud of turning some prisoners to Tavabs in the Bushehr prison, especially those who had not repented in other prisons. Sometimes, Tavabs would gather in the yard and surround a prisoner, and I could hear them hitting him.

Every now and then, Hamid Arab would come and take me to the interrogation room while having the same pyjamas on and would insult me. Hamid Arab did his best to insult the prisoners in any way he could, and he would physically hit the prisoners at every opportunity, and he would be happy. One day, he took me to the interrogator, and the interrogator said that my case was ongoing, but they didn't have a Hakem-e-Shar (religious judge). As soon as the Hakem-e-Shar (religious judge) came to Bushehr, I would go to court and be tried, which was good news, and I would get out of this uncertain situation.

I had trouble going to the bathroom or the yard every day with the ward guard, which sometimes would lead to a physical argument, which of course, would end in slaps or punches on my abdomen or chest. The longer I was kept in solitary confinement, the weaker I became.

The jailers wanted to break me, and, in fact, they were successful. Nevertheless, on all occasions of the interrogation and discussion, I emphasized that I had worked with the syndicate and had never been with the majority Organization, and that if I had worked a little with them, it had been more emotionally with its members. The interrogator would always emphasize that I was a sick person, and they were doctors, and they had to treat me. They left me alone for a while, my plan was to exercise and read the books I had read before. I tried to keep myself busy, but being in solitary confinement had taken all my energy, and sometimes, I had a psychological attack that would continue by me shouting and hitting the cell door, and after that, they would come and hit me until I would become unconscious. I could feel that I had lost control on myself and my behaviour. I was not in a good situation mentally.

One day, it was very hot in the cell and at the same time, I could not eat breakfast, and I was very ill. I could not eat the lunch they brought. There was no hunger strike because I did not think about it at all. Maybe I had just forgotten that I could use my hunger strike to get some points from the jailer. When I did not eat lunch, the guard came angrily asked why I didn't eat. I said I was not feeling well and needed a doctor. He laughed and left. It took me a while to get worse.

I started running in that cell, which was about two meters by two meters, and I ran so much in the room that I was confused, and I started vomiting. No matter how many times I knocked on the door, the guard did not care. I took off all my clothes. I was wearing only underpants, and I started punching the door and the wall until I became unconscious. As I fell to the ground, I noticed that the door opened. The guard came in and kicked me to get up. I started cursing, and he started beating me as hard as he could, and I was unconscious once again.

When I became conscious, I could feel pain in my entire body, and I was nauseous and dizzy. When I got up from the ground, I stumbled and could not control myself and fell. They brought dinner, but I could not get up. I just saw that he opened the cell and asked, as usual, if I wanted to go to the toilet. I did not even go to the toilet. I couldn't control my bladder because of the terrible beating I received from the guard. After a short time, Akbaripour came and tried to make me feel better a little and told me to go to the bathroom and then have dinner. I could not walk either, but with the help of one of the guards, I went to the shower, and took a bath, and returned to my cell. But generally, I was not feeling well at all. I had pain in my body, especially, I could feel a severe pain in my side, and again, that terrible pain in my kidney was tangible.

I couldn't eat dinner again. In the night, the guard came and said go to toilet now as the cell door won't be opened until morning. I went to toilet suffering from severe pain in my kidney. The guard had heard me shouting from pain, so he opened the door quickly as he was afraid of me committing suicide. I was not even thinking about it anymore because I was not even able to think, and I had no strength to do so. He took me back to the cell. I again started to run in the cell in the hope of decreasing my pain or even becoming unconscious to get rid of the pain. I vomited several times that night. The guard wouldn't care at all. I was feeling like I was dying that night. No energy was left in me.

Early in the morning, the guard opened the cell door and said it was time for going to the toilet and saying prayers. He knew that I wouldn't pray. I told him that I need doctor, and I was dying from the kidney pain. He said go to the toilet, then he would take me to to doctor. In the toilet, all of a sudden, I felt dizzy and fell on the floor.

The guards dragged me back to the cell with the help of someone else. I had fallen to the ground when the door opened, and someone came in and I couldn't understand who he was. I just remember that he gave me two pills and with a little water I drank, then I fell asleep very well. When I woke, I was lying naked on the floor with only a pair of pants on.

I started shouting again, and I kept punching the door of the cell. The guard came once again and made me quiet by beating me. I started to run in the cell again. I had no energy, so I could barely even run, and I would fall on the floor every now and then. I had not eaten lunch, and I had not gone to the toilet either. I had no more energy. I do not know why I would run in that small cell environment. All I knew was that running would reduce my kidney pain, make me dizzy, and make me fall to the ground. Until the evening I kept doing the same thing, I kept knocking at the door and the wall, I kept shouting. In the evening, the cell door was opened again, and I kept shouting. They started to kick me again, and after that, they took dinner for me and two pills. I took the pills, and after a while, it soothed my pain and I fell asleep. I couldn't feel anything anymore. It was midnight when I woke again due to my pain, and I kept walking in the cell, and I fell on the ground several times. But I stopped yelling and shouting, especially since I had a laryngeal problem, and when I would shout or speak loudly, my laryngeal fibers would become sensitive, and I would lose the ability to speak. I felt like I was suffocating. Now my shout was just a slow sound from my larynx. In the morning, with the help of the guard, I went to the bathroom, and afterwards, had some breakfast with tea. I lay down and fell asleep.

After a while, I woke due to a terrible pain in my kidney, and again, I started to run in the cell, shouting and knocking on the walls and the door. One of the violent officials of the prison whose name was Zende Budi came and made me quiet by beating me. In the evening, I felt bad. I lay on the floor. I had no energy to move anymore. I remember that a guard came and kicked me, but I had even no energy to move. In the evening, some other guys entered the ward, and I clearly remember that their leader was a person whose name was Nabi Mallahzade. He was the judge of the Revolutionary Court of Bushehr.

He was from Shokri neighbourhood and had moved from Khark with his family to Bushehr; Mohammad Saghiri and Iraj Saghiri were his uncles, and he and his brothers were good football players and as we were from a same neighbourhood, in the fifties we were friends and even we would sometimes exchange books with each other. I had got the book 53 Nafar by Bozorg Alavi from him and had read that as well. They entered my cell. I couldn't move at all; he kicked me in the side and asked if I was still alive. He stepped on my head and started pushing, and asked why I act like that, did I want to deceive them.

"Do you think I can let you out of here alive"? Others were just around me. I was lying on the floor of the cell. Nabi Malahzadeh was constantly cursing me while pressing his feet on my head; he told others that I was just acting, and they should let me die there! I could not even speak, and I could not speak because of the pressure on my throat. As Nabi Malahzadeh had his foot on my head, he was explaining my past to his companions and told them that I deserved to die there. I do not know how long it took him to stop putting his foot on my head.

They all left there, and again, the cell door was closed. After some time, Nabi Malahzadeh and his companions came to the cell once again.

They talked with each other for a while. I had no energy even to move. I could just hear them talking, and they were thinking what to do about me. Meanwhile, Nabi Malahzadeh came to me and again stepped on my head.

I had such a hard time, but I survived all those difficulties. One day, at 9 p.m., two guards came and told me to get up and go to the public ward. It may have been good news, but it was not good news due to what I had heard from the interrogator about the public ward. Whatever, it was better than this cell. Public ward four was actually behind the solitary confinement cells. I was lifted with difficulty in walking, and as I was dragged on the ground, they took me to the public ward.

This ward was well known as the Island Ward. There were also some prisoners there accused of financial crimes.

Many dangerous addicted prisoners were transferred from Tehran to an island near Asaluyeh. They were known as the islandis, and it was regularly broadcasted on the news that many addicts and dangerous prisoners had been sent into exile in the islands of Bushehr. On the island, they were left to fend for themselves, many of whom had died in this process, which was met with protest, and some of whom were transferred to Helali Prison, where they were kept and used in various works, and according to them, their imprisonment would last until the Mahdi Revolution (the 12th imam of Muslims), which means that if the Mahdi appears They will also be released, which meant somehow being in prison forever.

They were mostly talented in the arts. They were usually busy with painting in prison, and they had painted some of the wall paintings in the city about revolution and also pictures of those who had been killed in war, from Bushehr. On the other hand, some ordinary prisoners were there that their crime case was related to getting lots of urban lands from the government before the revolution, which was considered illegal.

In fact, it was like they took my corpse there as I could hardly even move. They laid me on the ground and left. At the same time, Zendebudi who was one of the guards and the prison authorities, called a person whose name was Davoud,and said that I was not allowed to talk to anybody and the point that I was only able to talk with Davoud. Over there, I got to see two people who were familiar to me among the prisoners: Mr Beladi, then governor of Khormuj, and Abbas Goshtasbi, who used to work in the school's laboratory and also construction fields. They laid me on the floor and left, and all the prisoners gathered around me and brought me a drink, which was very tasty, and Mr Beladi and Mr Goshtasbi were very kind.

As I laid on the floor, everyone was trying to do something for me. It was not long before Zendebudi entered the ward and they all scattered, except Davoud, who oversaw the room, sat next to me. As I was lying down, he started giving me some instructions that I was forbidden to talk or go to the exercise yard, and if I needed anything, I should talk to Davoud, and he left the ward.

Davoud made a place for me next to him; they helped me to stand. In total, there were 20 prisoners in the ward four. I leaned against the wall and sat.

They brought me food, and everyone sympathized with me with their gestures and looks without talking. There was a lights- out at ten o'clock, and everyone had to go to sleep, and I talked to Davoud about letting me take a shower after the lights-out because I had not taken a bath for a long time and my body was dirty. No one disagreed, and I went to the bathroom and took a bath and they added that in the morning, one of the prisoners who was from Mashhad would trim my beard and hair. I felt that I had entered heaven that night.

Most of the prisoners wouldn't pray, and that had made it easier for me to spend time there. I asked Davoud to let me help them with things needed to be done in the room and he said not to worry, for now I didn't need to do anything.

At night, everyone would lay their blankets and sleep, and in the morning, they would gather all blankets and lean them against the wall and would sit there, and those who had to work outdoors would be taken outside, and the rest of them would be busy doing things inside the prison, and some would paint. They would draw pictures of those killed in the war,on the canvas. A few days later, they took Mr Goshtasbi and Mr Beladi out of the prison. Maybe they were released. I could just say good bye with my eyes as I was not allowed to talk to anyone. After a few days of having adequate food, sleep, bathing, and rest, I regained my strength, and through David, I got permission from the prisoners to exercise in the ward for a half hour a day, if possible. The prisoners had no problem with it, and everyone in the ward was doing their own thing, and they let me exercise in the afternoon that others would go to the yard and the ward was empty.

A few days later, one of the prisoners who was painter, had noticed that I would look at him passionately while he was painting, spoke to me with Davoud's permission and said if I wanted to learn, I would ask the prison for extra supplies and teach me painting, which was a good opportunity. I could learn painting. I started working on the canvas with the explanations he gave me. Of course, we were not allowed to talk with each other, so in fact, he would give all explanations to me, and I would just listen to him. Without talking to each other. A few days later, I was summoned to the interrogation room. Of course, Hamid Arab was standing outside. When I went outside the ward, he took my hand and dragged me to the interrogator. The interrogator started talking about Islam and the role of liberty on people and continued telling me I was a Muslim in the past, not so today and how it had happened to me to become a communist?. Of course, he just wanted to speak without listening, so I was just a listener there. He said take off the blindfold, and I took it off. He was a young boy who knew all my family members, and he said do you need anything? I asked for books, and I added that I had been waiting for a trial for a long time. He said that we do not have a Hakem Sharie (a religious judge) now. They gave me a number of books on the history of Islam to read.

STUDYING THE HISTORY OF ISLAM

I started to study the history of Islam; a Tavab would give the books to me. He was one of the Mujahed Tavabs who was allowed to enter ward four and give me the books. I stopped learning to paint, and instead, I started to study about Islam history, which was so good. Still, I was not allowed to go to the exercise yard. I asked several times until they accepted my request to go to the yard two times per week alone. which was a great for me. Ordinary prisoners were also mostly busy doing their personal things; each would entertain himself in a particular way. One day, at lunch time, we had an eggplant dish. Unlike other prisoners, they only gave me a little bit of eggplant and rice without any meat in it. I asked the person who was in charge of the room about the reason, but he didn't care, so I got angry. I messed everything up, and I faced with other prisoners' protest. One of them said I was not allowed to speak. I said ask the person in charge of the room to explain why there was no meat or eggplant in my food unlike the others. If I stayed quiet, it didn't mean they could do whatever they want.

One of the prisoners got up and approached me to have a physical confrontation, but Davoud didn't let him get close to me and tried to calm the situation. One of the prisoners from Mashhad said he had been in prison much longer than me; who did I think I was to disrupt the calm atmosphere. I answered, "I'm not allowed to talk, but if I say something, I'm ready for any of the consequences". And again, I asked the same question about my food. I said you guys don't know anything about me. I have been in prison more than anybody else here. I asked the guy from Mashhad how long he had been in prison, He answered that he used to have a hotel and was originally from Mashhad, and he continued that he had been in different prisons for many years. I said, me too. He asked which prison II was in. said I was in Shiraz prison in 1353(1975). He was surprised and asked if I knew Ghasem Jafari? I said, yes, of course. I continued that when I was in solitary confinement, he helped me a lot. I have been in the same solitary confinement with many popular people that he knew, and I named some of them; they all knew those people. Almost all prisoners changed their point of view about me after that night as they had understood that I was not just one of those new prisoners, so they would respect more, especially considering the situation I was in when they took me to prison. After the whole thing, I apologised them for disturbing the calm atmosphere, and by doing so, I put an end to all those things. At night, Zendebudi came to the ward and called me. I went out. He said why I spoke when I was told not to. He started punching and kicking me, and my mouth was full of blood.

He threatened me that in the morning I had to answer to the authorities about breaking the rules. I went back to the ward while my mouth was bleeding. After taking shower, other prisoners brought me a drink, and without talking, they tried to calm me. In the morning, Akbaripour called me to go to his office. We talked for few minutes, and I made a commitment to follow the rules of the prison. We didn't have any physical confrontation.

One day, several political prisoners were brought to ward four. It was like exam sessions; they sat in line on the floor, and each of them had some paper and a pen and they would write some items. Before that, one of the Tavabs' members whose name was Abdullah Arabzade who was one of the Mujahedin's supporters and had become Tavab and interrogator assist in the prison, came to the ward and told me if I knew any of the people that would come to the ward, I was not allowed to talk with them or even look at them. "You will just wait until they leave the ward".

I knew some of them, but I kept my head down, not to look at them and made myself busy with books. Among them, I knew Fazel Namir well. He was arrested in 1355(1976) in Bushehr with his friend Mohammad Darvish, who were both from Deylam, and they came to Ward four and were in prison for some time. After the revolution, his friend Mohammad Darvish became the interrogator of the Revolutionary Guards, and Fazel became one of the Mujahedin Khalq activists, the interrogator of Fazel Namir was his friend Mohammad Darvish.

Fazel was executed in 1367(1989). They filled in the sheets, and one by one, they handed the sheets to Abdullah Arab Zadeh and.

One day, when I was alone in the yard, suddenly, a guard came and dragged me to the ward and left me there. Later, it was reported that in ward five, a 16-year-old Mujahedin's supporter had set himself on fire with kerosene and died. The reason was that he had been raped and this had led to his suicide.

I continued studying the history of Islam, and from time to time, I was summoned by the interrogator, and he would talk for a while and, in fact, he was trying to get to know me and my ideas more. Based on my experience, I was fully aware of his movements. I was in ward four; I could bear the prison more easily. But that didn't mean t the pressures of the past few months had not affected me. I was among the island prisoners. One day, a guard came and told me to pack my stuff as they were going to move me to another ward. I thanked the prisoners in ward four and went to the new ward. When I came out of ward four, the guard said I was going to be transferred to ward five. I entered ward five. The person in charge of the ward was a Tavab whose name was Mustafa Sabzi, a supporter of the Mujahedin, and the ideological political leader of the Khosravi ward, who was a member of the Revolutionary Guards, and later, he was arrested for infiltration.

Fortunately, there I found Fazlullah-K and I had the chance to be besides him at night.

It was like Shiraz here. Early in the morning after breakfast, different and intensive classes were held, but there was much more rest. On the other hand, it was ordered that I was not allowed to talk with others in the yard; and the point that I was only allowed to talk with the prisoners of ward five. There were some Tavabs who would come to me and after walking and talking for a while; they would insult and threaten me, and they would leave there after that. I would just listen to them without being allowed to answer them back. If I talked, I would be punished.

Once, when I was walking in the yard one of the Tavabs of ward five started insulting me and threatened that I wouldn't get out of there alive, and after that, he left there.

On the entrance door of the ward they had written all prisoners' names with the crime cases they had been arrested for. That guy's name was Bahreini, and he was a supporter of the Majority. There were two brothers who had been arrested for supporting the Communist Union.

They were in Room five and his brother was arrested in Tehran, and they had been transferred to Bushehr. Abdullah Arab Zadeh came to the prison one day with a group of Tavabs and surrounded those two brothers and started talking about dialectics and mocking, and they said that the communists share their sisters and mothers and wives with others to enjoy them, and they asked them why they don't do that. Tavabs only wanted to find a weak point in the prisoners who just wanted to end their imprisonment and be released from prison and attack them.

One day, as I was walking, I saw that Abdullah Arab Zadeh went to Javad Granbaha, who was one of the famous football players of Bushehr and was arrested at that time for smuggling carpets, and slapped him. Javad Granbaha saw me for a moment. Of course, I tried to pretend like I had not seen anything. Javad knew me well, and at that moment, I felt how embarrassed he must have been to be treated like this. Life was very difficult for everyone except Tavabin. One day, Tavabs went to a young prisoner who was one of Mujahedin supporters and beat him. They said that he had had a gun and had not said anything about it during interrogation. He was one of the so-called telephone arrests.

Telephone arrests were those who would enter an organization without knowing that those organisations were organized by the Revolutionary Guards. They would be tricked by a phone number, which was given to them to go meet a person of the organisation, who in fact was their interrogator. One morning, they called me to get dressed and come out. I thought it was court, and I was happy because I could get rid of that uncertain situation. I went to the head of the prison's office, they handcuffed me and led me to a Peikan car; the interrogator was in that car as well. The interrogator laughed and said he wanted to make me happy.

Behind the Fanoos cinema, there was one of the intelligence service offices, they took me inside and told me to sit there and not move! A few minutes later, Mehrnoosh and her mother entered the room. The interrogator said to think about this child's future. I saw Mehrnoosh after a few years. They let me hug Mehrnoosh. I was happy for some minutes that Mehrnoosh was beside me. I told the interrogator that he knew very well that I had nothing to do with the Organisation and their activities.

He said he hoped I would be released soon. Mehrnoosh's mother said that she had written a letter to Mosayebi, the ruler of Shiraz; she had found some acquaintances who had promised her to release me and said that Mehrnoosh was ill, and we had to take her to doctor as soon as possible to treat her. She was explaining Mehrnoosh's illness to the interrogator. I was put in the same car and taken back to the prison.

I went back to ward five. I was summoned to the interrogator's room several times, and his focus was more on political issues; he asked for my opinion. I said I was not theoretically strong, and I did not have much time to study outside. The interrogator just wanted to talk a little and show strength and leave after that.

One day, Abdullah Arab Zadeh came and took me to the interrogator's room and put a few white sheets in front of me and asked me to draw the organizational chart of the Majority. I said as I had never got involved in those issues. I had no idea about it, but I added that I could give them some information about Metal and Mechanics and the Metalworker and Mechanics Housing office in which I was active. I went back to room five.

It was not long before I was taken to the interrogation room, and I explained to them that I needed a doctor and that I was very ill and asked them to send me to the court as soon as possible. The interrogator promised that they would do so as soon as possible because Bushehr did not yet have a religious ruler by then.

The interrogator promised that my future situation would be clear as soon as possible, and I returned to the ward. With some insults from Abdullah Arab Zadeh, it became the visiting day, and I was getting visitors for the first time in Bushehr prison. Tavabs were all gathered in the hall; they all went to the yard with slogans in favour of Khomeini, revolution and death to the hypocrites and infidels. There were several cabins outside being used as visiting rooms. I heard the chants of death to the hypocrites, death to the infidels, and chants about Khomeini. It was a very bad scene because it showed the visitors that everyone in prison had changed their idea by force, and they were defending Khomeini and his government.

For the first time since I had entered ward five, I visited my mother. She said that she had met Mr Nabavi, and he had promised to do his best to release me from the prison. Mr Nabavi (Seyed Mohammad Hasan Nabavi was born in Chavoshi village, one of the villages of Dashti city, he represented Khobregan Ghanun Asasi [constitutional experts] and three parliamentary terms.) He was also my teacher back in school, he used to teach religion in 1351(1973) and knew me a little bit. Mom added that she also sent a request letter to the parliament and asked them to release me. After visiting her, I went back to the ward. Arab came and took me to the interrogator room. He talked about Khomeini and his role in world issues. Afterwards, I went back to the ward. Mom came to visit me once again and emphasized that she was trying to release me from the prison through Mr Nabavi.

One day, they summoned me to the interrogator room. And they said that I needed to make a commitment, and I said that's okay, no problem. I was under a lot of pressure, and I just wanted to be released from that hell.

Another problem was the point that I was not allowed to exercise alone, as all prisoners should have taken part in the exercise sessions, which was led by Tavabs; in those sessions, they would chant slogans about those who were against the revolution. And if a person didn't take part in those sessions, he would be considered as an anti-revolution prisoner.

One day, Abdullah Arab Zadeh came and said put on your clothes, we need to go out. I put on my clothes quickly, and we went to the interrogator. He said that my case was pending, and soon, the final verdict would come. He added to go and take care of my family, and I went back to the ward. I talked with Fazlullah. He said that I was most probably going to be released soon.

After some time, Arab Zadeh came and said you I had to go to the court.

We went to the head of the prison's room with Abdullah Arab Zadeh. There, with two guards, we went to a Peikan car and to the Revolutionary Court. When I got to court, I saw my mother standing in front, and she looked happy. We entered the Revolutionary Court. The interrogator was standing waiting for me. He said that since they didn't have a religious ruler at the moment, I would be released with a commitment until the religious ruler came. He also added that I needed to go to the headquarters regularly to let them know about my situation, and I said that I had no problem with that. Some other prisoners had been released exactly like that in Shiraz as well. Later, I met one of my friends who had been released under the same condition as well.

I waited in court, and after few minutes, I went to the second floor. The prosecutor's office, where Tashkori was there. He talked a lot about Mujahedin's situation abroad, the second revolution, and the point that various political forces were not united anymore, and the fact that the Islamic revolution was the correct thing. I was released on bail, the house deed , I went out of the court.

Outside the Revolutionary Court, my mom and older sister were waiting for me. Before leaving the court, the prosecutor came to me once again and expressed his happiness that I was released.

Earlier, I had promised to go to the headquarters the next morning. I went with my mother and my sister to their house. Family members were waiting for me.

I was mentally disturbed and had lost my focus on things going around me and could not bear to sit in public, and as soon as I had lunch, I went to bed and slept.

The next morning, I went to the headquarters, and I asked them for a permission to go to Shiraz, as that was where,I used to live. They promised that after few days they would let me go to Shiraz and go to the headquarters there. Once, I met the interrogator again. He expressed his happiness again and said he had a cinema ticket for a movie by Mohsen Makhmalbaf and recommended I go watch that movie.

The film was about the prisoners in during the Shah Kingdom. I got the ticket and walked from the headquarters to the Fanoos Cinema, which was a short distance away. At headquarters, I explained about Mehrnoosh's illness and that I had to go to Shiraz as soon as possible and take Mehrnoosh to the doctor, and the interrogator said that there was no problem, and I could go to Shiraz.

I went to Shiraz with my mom, and as soon as I arrived, I went to the dormitory for war victims, a place in which Mehrnoosh, her mother, and her brother used to live; I decided to take her to a specialist as soon as possible. I went to the metalworking workshop in Fakhrabad, the place I had been arrested, and they welcomed me warmly. I talked with

H about Mehrnoosh's illness. He called a doctor and managed to make an appointment with a specialist.

I went to the doctor, and after the examination, I explained to him that part of my leave from prison was due to her illness..He examined her carefully and wrote a prescription; he did not get money for his visit and introduced me to the pharmacy not to pay for the prescription. When we returned home with Mehrnoosh, her mother explained that she had written letters to the Revolutionary Court explaining Mehrnoosh's illness and demanded my release. Of course, in the prison when she came to see me, she was told that it was not clear when I would be released.

After meeting them few times, I explained that due to several problems including being unemployed, the mental situation that I had, and some other problems, I couldn't live with anybody, and I asked her to marry if she found a good person. There were tough economic situations in those days. My shoes were torn, and I couldn't afford to buy a new pair of shoes, and I didn't want to borrow money from anybody else. One day, when I went to meet them, some women who were related to the war victim's foundation were there. We talked for a while, and finally, they said that she was going to get married again and told me that it was better for me not to go there anymore. I found it logical; I didn't meet them anymore.

SPENDING TIME IN CEMETERIES
AND SLEEPING IN GRAVES

I was looking for a job for a while, but I could not find a job because it was psychologically difficult for me to work. The only source of income for the house was the little money my sister would earn. She used to work in a laboratory with my little brother, and they were paid a little. A very close friend of "H" who was in Fakhrabad told me many times that if I did not have money, he would lend some to me, but I did not accept. I was mentally exhausted, and I would only walk in the city in the mornings until I got tired and returned home. Gradually, I would go more often to the cemetery. In the morning, I would go to the cemetery and spend my time there. So, I spent most of my time in the cemetery, after that I would go more often to Morde Shur Khune (a place where they wash dead bodies before burying them). I would stand and look at them for hours while they were washing corpses before burying them. Sometimes, I would also help them to wash the dead bodies and help them to bury them.

I was in the cemetery all the time. Some nights, I would sleep there. The committee based in the cemetery would not object if I slept there at night.

Gradually, I became a person who would help them in Shiraz Cemetery. Sometimes, my hand would swell, and I could feel a severe pain. I would go to hospital but they would not help me.

One day, I noticed that my left eyelid was swollen and had completely covered my eye, and I had severe pain and pus. It was so swollen that I could not see anything out of my left eye, and my right eye was also swollen. I had a very severe pain with a headache when I went to the hospital, but unfortunately, they didn't help me. I decided to visit a private doctor. I went to visit Dr. "H", who was one of the imprisoned doctors of the Shah's Kingdom. The office was in a very good location.

I went there and said I wanted to see the doctor. The woman sitting at the table looked at me and asked sceptically, "Why do you want to see the doctor"? I told him that I was one of his friends, and I asked her to tell the doctor that Naser from Bushehr has come to see him.

She went and informed the doctor; he came and hugged me and with a surprised look asked what happened. He asked his secretary to not send any other patients inside while I was being examined. I explained the entire story to him; he was sorry. He started examining me, and he continued that this is a dangerous virus and gave me an ointment that was temporary anaesthesia and emphasized that the ointment should not get into my eyes, and it was very annoying. He wrote the prescription and said to get it from a particular pharmacy, and he also said that I did not need to pay for the prescription. He set another appointment for me and left.

After a short time, he returned and gave me an envelope. After thanking him, I left his office. He asked me to promise him not to go to the cemetery anymore and to go to the park instead of the cemetery and try to spend my time in the park.

The next time I had an appointment with the doctor, he referred me to a psychiatrist who was one of his friends. He said that I didn't need to pay, and that doctor, who was also a psychologist, gave me all the anti-stress and anti-depressant pills and emphasized that I should not go to the cemetery under any circumstances. With the emphasis of both doctors, I started exercising and walking, and I also used the pills from the psychologist.

I went to Fakhrabad to meet that friend "H"; I explained to him all I had gone through from going to cemetery to visiting the psychologist. He got so upset. His brother had just been released from Evin.

His brother used to study in India and was arrested on his return. He had been imprisoned for a long time in Evin, and H himself was a graduate of India. They gave me a temporary job there; this way I could stay busy so that my mental condition would improve until I could find a better job.

They would give me a little money on the weekends, which was very useful for me psychologically in general. I went to Bushehr with the permission of the headquarters. I told my friends that I was unemployed and looking for a job. I did not go to the headquarters for a while. I saw that they were not sensitive, and gradually, I would go to the headquarters rarely. I returned to Shiraz. My friend, who had been hiding for some time, had been released from prison and had a metalworking workshop in one of the cities of Fars Province, and he had a job and needed help. We went together and did his work, which was a good help both psychologically and financially, but he sold the workshop as he was going to continue his studies in the university. I went back to Bushehr and started to look for finding another job.

In Bushehr, my friends suggested that in Khormoj there was a metalworking workshop, and I could work there. It was a good offer. Khormoj is in the southeast of Bushehr and the centre of Dashti City, and its climate is hot and dry. Its people speak in Persian with Dashti Khormuj dialect.

I went to Khormuj and to my friend's workshop. I spent the night at their house and decided to find a room to start working in their workshop. I found a single room and started working in that workshop. It was good financial help, and it helped me a lot psychologically. On the other hand, I was far from Bushehr and Shiraz, and I stopped taking the pills. I worked in Khormuj for a long time. One day, I went to Khormuj market to shop when I came across one of the prison's Tavabs. He was one of the Tavabs of the Mujahedin. I saw him, and he came and asked how I was and what I was doing there. I said I work in a workshop; I bought some stuff and went to my room. I went back to the workshop and explained what happened to my friend; I had seen one of the prison's Tavabs. He said go home and do not stay in the workshop today, and he asked me just to cook food that night. I was cooking dinner when one of the workers of the workshop came to me and said to quickly go to the workshop.

I went to the workshop and my friend said that some people had come there from the headquarters; they had asked them to inform me that I had to go there as soon as possible.

The workshop was not so far from IRGC, so I decided to go on foot. There was a young man in the headquarters; I told him that I work in the metalwork workshop. I said he asked my employer to let me come here as soon as possible. He was a polite man unlike Bushehr; he said I must have informed the headquarters that I was going to work in this city. With a little bit of threatening, which was a typical thing about the intelligence service, he asked me several questions like how did I find work there and why I work there. Then they said I are not allowed to stay in this city, and I should leave, and after that, I needed to go to Bushehr's headquarter. I stayed there until 8 p.m., and afterwards, they added that tomorrow I had to go to Bushehr, and they asked me to give a commitment not to go back to that city again.

The next day, I went to Bushehr and to the Bushehr headquarters. They asked why I went to Khormuj without permission. "Weren't you supposed to inform us wherever you go"? I was supposed to go to the headquarters every day. After that, I went to a friend's house and told him about it, and I was at his house for a while, and I lived at my uncle and sister's house for some time as well. But after a few days, they said that I did not need to come to headquarters. I returned to Shiraz. I decided to go to my mother's cousin's, who had a trailer. I travelled to many cities of Iran by trailer with him, and at the same time, I learned to drive a trailer, which could be my next job, but after few weeks I told him that this job is not suitable for me. I thanked him, and I became unemployed again.

BECOMING A MEMBER OF METALWORKERS' BOARD OF DIRECTORS

··

I returned to Bushehr to ask my friends for help finding a job. A friend of mine suggested that I could go to Choghadak and start a metalworking workshop. He added that they will help too. I said I went to Khormuj, and I was expelled from the city.

Now you are telling me to go to Choghadak to apply for a workshop permit? I wrote a letter and applied for a permit for a metalworking workshop in Choghadak and went to the governor's office because Choghadak was under the supervision of the Bushehr governor. Choghadak is a city in Bushehr province and is located on the road from Bushehr to Borazjan during World War One when Britons attacked Iran, Ghazanfar-Olsaltane and his allies defended the city against them, that war became well known as Choghadak War). In the morning, I went to the governor's office to apply for a metalworking permit. The governor of Bushehr was one of the reactionary Muslims who was imprisoned during Pahlavi dynasty and was thirsty for the blood of the communists. I had no choice but to go to the governor's office. I was waiting in a room when a man came and said, "Do you want to work in a metalworking workshop in Choghadak"? I said yes. He took my letter to the governor, and after few minutes, he came back and gave me the signed letter and that said I needed to go to Bakhshdari (office in charge of small cities) now and they would issue my permit.

My friend and I went to Choghadak Bakhshdari the same day and I showed them the letter, which was welcomed, and they asked for a series of documents that I had to prepare. My friend and I returned to Bushehr, and I prepared the necessary documents and a work permit was issued. I also found a shop that was great for work, and I promised the shop owner that I would hire his son as a co-worker. The owner of the shop was a war immigrant who had managed to work there and had several shops. It was time to buy tools, and that required a lot of money. The owner of the shop said I didn't need to pay rent until I started working.

Everything was ready. Now I had to buy metalworking tools that I had no money for. Gholam, who was a very close friend of mine and had always helped me in difficult times, came to me and lent me 90,000 tomans, which I was supposed to return after starting to work there. I quickly went to Fakhrabad. Nasser, who had a workshop in Fakhrabad and had many friends in Tehran, helped me, and I was able to order all the necessary tools. Due to having the official work permit, my friends added me as a member to the Metalworkers' Cooperative and my iron sheet quota was taken from the cooperative, which was a quite great financial help for me. Back then, every metalwork workshop would get a quota of iron sheets from the Metalworkers' Cooperation under the supervision of the Commercial Department.

The tools and all the equipment of the workshop were purchased from Tehran and transferred to Bushehr. I started working there. I also rented a room in the house of the shop owner to stay in the city of Choghadak and live in that room.

I received the quota of iron sheets. I would work every day and stayed in Choghadak most of the nights. One day, I was summoned by Bakhshdari, I went there.

Despite almost every time I was greeted by the Bakhsdar (the head of the Bakhshdari), this time he greeted me angrily and asked why I didn't say I had been in prison. He said that I was no longer allowed to stay in the city. I had to return to Bushehr after 6 p.m. Anyway, I handed over the room and went to Bushehr, rented a room, and in the mornings, I would go to Choghadak and return to Bushehr in the afternoon. At six o'clock in the afternoon, a Basiji motorcyclist would come to watch the shop, as I had to return to Bushehr at six o'clock in the afternoon.

It was the Bushehr Metalworkers' Cooperative election, and I also became a candidate for it, and they started the election day in the presence of the representative of the city cooperative.

During this time, I had received a lot of information from the cooperative that the workshops licensed by the Department of Industries and Mines would also receive quotas from the quota of those who had also received licenses from the municipality. I argued that workshops licensed from industries and mines should not use the quotas of those who receive quotas from the municipality, and it was generally argued that a vote was taken, and I got the most votes and became a member of the cooperative board. I focused on the fact that we should cut the quotas for large industrial workshops related to industry and divide that among the other members. I also moved the cooperative office to another location. The Commercial Office would also send their representative to the office because the cooperative quota was issued by the Commercial Office.

Mohammad Halilei, who was the representative of the Commercial Department, cooperated with me a lot and I managed to cut the iron mafia out of the cooperative, and I also changed the company's articles of association and distributed the quotas of the cities fairly.

The cooperative had complete control over the workshops so that no one's rights were lost.

We coordinated with Mohammad Halilei that the main part of metalworking products should be exported through Hawaleh (bill of exchange) Commercial Office so that everyone could buy their metal supplies at a fair price. The city cooperative also supported me; I would support the consumers, and we struck a balance between black market and government prices. These changes that took place in the cooperative, the big workshop owners, who used to also receive the quota of the Industrial Administration and the deputy, started trying to not let me continue working in the cooperation, making excuses such as I was in prison and should not be on the board, and my conflict with them was getting worse and worse day by day. They tried their best to fire me from the board. While continuing my work in Choghadak, I was also actively involved in the cooperative. On the other hand, in the workshop of Choghadak, everything was going really well, and we had made a great progress. I also asked the Bakhshdari (an office in charge of small cities) to let me stay in Choghadak and work in the workshop until 9 or 10 p.m., providing I went back to Bushehr after that and not staying in the city; the cooperative was also in the right way, and opposition would also try to disturb our activities in the cooperative office.

Of course, the city cooperative also agreed and supported my work. One day when I went to Shiraz, I heard about the execution of several prisoners, but I did not believe it. The news was not clear; the only thing which was clear was the fact that several prisoners had been executed in prison. I returned to Bushehr and continued working in both the workshop and the cooperative as well. Opposition gathered a number of shopkeepers and tried to create a physical confrontation, which was resolved by talking and explaining the cooperative work.

I demanded that the General Assembly convene all the members of the cooperative and vote on the articles of association that I had written. I took some copies of the articles of association and gave them to the members of the cooperative to study to be informed of the text of the articles of association on the day of the assembly.

Ahmad S. and I went to the house of Dariush Barghak, who was a supporter of the Mujahedin, and Ahmad informed me of his execution, and we went to their house together. This was followed by the news of the execution of Mehdi Sheshbolooki and the news of several other executions that were all carried out during the Shahrivar 1367 (the September 1988) murders.

During this time, I met a person named Mr Eidan, who was a war immigrant and had a company in Tangak in the Bushehr industrial zone. When I said I was going to Shiraz, he also travelled with me, and we talked a lot on the way about different issues, especially he asked some questions about the articles of association, and I explained to him.

He needed a set of tools, so we went to Fakhr Abad together and introduced him to my friends there, and they provided him with all things he needed. As time went by, our friendship became stronger.

I gave the quotas given to us by the Department of Commerce to the trade unions, and I gave the quotas of the industrial workshops to the Department of Industries and Mines. That turned out to be a few acute clashes between them and me. A letter was sent from the intelligence service that I had to be fired from the board. Several members who opposed me we happy, and I was fired from the board. I went to Choghadak, and I continued working there.

I had two workers who I insured, and I got a social security booklet and gave it to them. Mr Eidan suggested that we could go to his workshop in Tangak and visit his workshop, which I was happy to do, and we went there together. Of course, his company wasn't working in Tangak, and there were only two industrial sheds there. I said that if he did not work there, how did he get the quota? We went to Shiraz together. On the way, he offered me a partnership in his company. He said, first close the workshop in Choghadak and take the tools and bring them there and we can do great things. The offer was great, and I accepted, and it was decided to establish a new company. I suggested that we name it Lahmir, which means transformative, and it was the name of the wind that blew in the fall, which was very dangerous, and the dinghies would not leave the port unless they were sure that those winds were not going to blow anymore. The company with the same name was registered under the name of Bushehr Lahmir. Eidan and M. and I were on the board of directors; we started working. I wrote the company's articles of association, and I registered as CEO. For the first time, we boarded a plane and went to Tehran to register and publish it in the company's newspaper. Mr Eidan had many connections with various sections, which helped us to be successful in our field.

We employed a lot of workers, and we insured all of them and we managed the work successfully. Until, unfortunately, Eidan died of cancer; it had a profound effect on our work. We also regularly received remittances through the Commercial Office. After the death of Mr Eidan, Mohammad Halilei, who sincerely supported us because he saw that we were working honestly, was also fired from the Commercial Office for a reason that I never asked him. Mohammad Halilei and his family did not cut his relationship with me during the time I was under pressure, even though he was under pressure as well to not communicate with me, and he supported me all the time. One day, I received a letter from the Revolutionary Court that was a summons, and I had to introduce myself to the Revolutionary Court. I told Mohammad Halilei about it, and he said not to worry. The next day, I went to the Revolutionary Court and showed the summons. They said I should go to the corner where there was a building and also the intelligence office. I went there, and they said that today we have a religious judge, and the interrogator came and said to come inside. I went in, and the interrogator talked to someone. He said he hoped I would not be sentenced to prison and will be released, and then I was taken to the courtroom. Many people with different crimes were gathered there. They would read each person's name, and they would leave the courtroom after a few minutes. They called me around three in the afternoon. I went inside; a mullah was sitting at the table, and I only knew the interrogator among them. There were a lot of files on the mullahs' table. He looked at my file and asked my surname. He continued that the communist vision had disappeared, and he said that the communist foreign minister had kissed Mr Khomeini's hand. He said that the Soviet Union had disappeared. He did not ask any questions about my case. Then he said go... That's it, and my trial was over. I left the court. After few days, I told Mohammad Halilei that our house was mortgaged to the bank.

A few days later, he informed me that I could get the house deed back. I also went to the Revolutionary Court, and there they gave me a letter to go to the judiciary and release the house deed, and there I raised the issue of my sister who had made a commitment, which was also resolved, and in fact, I was released, and I had no obligation anymore and I was free now, and I could leave the country.

During this time, I was summoned to the headquarters only once or twice that was mostly about discussing political and global issues; in fact, they wanted to make sure that everything was okay.

With the agreement of the company's partners, I as one of the shareholders of the company transferred my equity to my brother, and I was no longer responsible in the company. Following that, I researched how I could get a passport without any possible problems from the intelligence service. One day, I went to the passport office and handed over the documents, and they told me to go to the National Bank and deposit the passport money and bring the receipt. I saw Ahmad at the National Bank. He said he had applied for a passport and was not allowed to leave. Now they have to repay the deposit for his passport. I said, so I might also be banned from leaving? He said maybe. I transferred the money to the passport office and handed the receipt to them.

One day, I went to the passport office, and they had issued my passport so I already a passport. The occupation of Kuwait by Iraq was over, and Kuwait government had started to issue work visa once again which was a good opportunity for me, so I asked my sister who used to live in Kuwait to get a Kuwaiti visa for me, and fortunately, a Kuwaiti work visa was issued and sent to me very quickly. I was ready to leave Iran, but at the same time, I had to be cautious about the intelligence service and things related to them. I went through all the processes normally needed to leave the country. I was just waiting for an opportunity to get a ticket and leave the country. I got a ticket to go from Bushehr to Kuwait by ship, and I got ready to move. During this time, I tried not to show up in the city that much not to face any problem. As time went by, the more excited and apprehensive I became about not getting arrested the day I was leaving the country.

During this time, I was supported by Mohammad Halilei; he kept telling me not to worry and there will be no problems. The day that I was waiting for came. I was supposed to leave Bushehr at 6 p.m. and arrived in Kuwait at 10 a.m. I had to go to customs at four o'clock, and my family were all worried about me outside there. Especially, considering the point that when you were on the ship, you could see them from the other side. The initial work was done, and we moved towards the ship; there was an intelligence agent checking passports. He looked at my passport and saw that I had a work visa. He handed me my passport; I went up the stairs of the ship. As I went upstairs, I looked at my family, who were looking at me anxiously. I waved to them; everything was over. I was still worried until the ship left. I felt the ship s hake gently and set off.

I was so anxious. After 15 years of living full of stress in Iran, I was leaving now, but an unknown fate awaited me. I came to the deck and watched Bushehr from there. I walked on the deck and went to the ship hall, and I went back to the deck again. I tried to control myself mentally. I tried to control myself by walking. When we reached the Khark area, they announced that the weather was a bit bad and the ship was shaking; they asked us to be more careful. I went to the deck and looked at Bushehr for the last time. At ten o'clock in the morning, I arrived at the port of Sheikh and set foot on Kuwaiti soil, and now I could wholeheartedly believe that I had come out of that hell.

I kept telling myself that I was born in exile, I was brought up in exile, and now I had to start a new life in exile.

LIST OF POLITICAL PRISONERS IN SHIRAZ FROM 1352 TO 1357

Ebrahim Avakh Ebrahim Afsorde
Del Ebad Ahmadzadeh Taghi
Afshani Ahmad Ahmadi Majid Amin
Moaiad Rahim Ansari Hosein
Akbaripour Emami
Mohammad Ebrahimzadeh Taher
Ahmadzadeh
Noruz Ahmadzadeh Ramezan
Asgharpour Changiz Ahmadian Bai
Morad Esfandiari Mahdi Eslami
Naser Aghajari Ramezan Azad
Majid Aghajani Khalu Ahmad
Ebrahim Ebrahimi Javad
Oskouei Arian Arianfar
Abdullah Amiri Hamid
Arzpeima
Maoud Esmaeilkhani Hooshidar
Eshraghi Mohammad Akbari
Ahmad Afshar
Reza Bakeri Mansour Bazargan
Ali Bolourian Samad Balaei
Mahmoud Badieh
Hesam Banihashemi Rahim Banaei
Iraj Bahrami Mansour
Bidar Alie Behpour
Abdullah Bidshahri Gholamhosein
Puzesh Abdullah Puzesh Khalil Pak Nia
Hadi Pakzad Javid Pashaei
Saeed Poorabdullah Rahmat
Pakdaman Ahmad Pouianfar
Ebrahim Pouianfar Mohammad

Piran Ahmad Taghdimi Hosein Tafreshi
Alimohammad Tashid Karim Taslimi
Nematullah Tagha Parviz
Jahanbakhsh Allahgholi Jahangiri
Abdullah Javidi Hassan Jafari
Kamran Changizadeh Abbas Hajari
Davoud Solhdust Mohammad Hoseini
Habibullah Habibi Kazem Hagh Shenas
Akbar Hadad Mohammad Haghighat
Homayoun Hajikhani Zeinodin Haghani
Mohammad sadegh Mohieddin Haieri
Fathullah Khamenei Hosein
Khoshnevis Mahdi Khosroshahi
Ardeshir Khandan Rahmat
Khoshkdaman Morad Khorshidi
Razi Khodadad Saeid
Dadsetan Morteza Danaei
Ali Dadgar Abbas Davari
Hooshang Delkhah Ahmad Dargahi
Mohammad Darvish Ebrahim Del
Afsordeh Darinanni
Ebrahim Dadvand Khalil Rezaei
Ali Mir Riahi Ali Rahimi
Bahman Radmerikhi Nooredin Riahi
Mohammad Ali Rahmani Taghi Razi
Nasrullah Ruhinezhad
Ahmad Riazi
Alireza Zomorrodian Ahmad
Zarkesh Faraj Sarkoohi
Ali Sarmadi
Seyyed Jalil Seyyed Ahmadian Ezzatullah Sahabi
Fariborz Sanjari Aziz
Sarmadi Abbas Surki Seifullahi
Hasan Saadati Mansoureh
Sinaei Reza Sotudeh
Mohammad Taghi Seyyed Ahmadi (Professor, Khaltourian)

Abdulhosein Soleimani Asghar
Shapourian Heshmatullah Shahrzad
Abdullah Shahbazi Kazem Shadvar
Mohammad Shalguni Alireza Shokuhi
Bahram Shalguni Nasser Sanaei
Esfandiar Sadeghzadeh Dariush Sanei
Ali Safaei
Asghar Sahranian
Rahim Sabouri Davoud Solhdust
Parviz Zarghami Abdulhosein Zarifi
Mohammad Rafi Ziaei
Mohammad Tabatabaei Rajab Ali Taheri
Hasan Taheripour Jafar
Abbaszadegan Ali Amouei
Saadi Alizadeh Esmaeil Abedi
Abdullah Ezzatpour Jafar
Abbaszadegan Aziz
Moeinie Araghi Aziz Ghaffari
Professor. Ghafour
Mahdi Ghabraei Rasoul Gheiratmand
Abdullah Gheiratmand Reza Farmahini
Ahmad Faghihi Abdullah Faghihi
Mohammad Faghihi Mohammad
Ferdosi Habib Farzad Khorshid Faghih
Fakhreddin Fani Ahmad Farhadi
Keramatullah Fahimi Fazelizadeh
Haj Fararouei Bahram Ghobadi
Abdullah Ghavami Parviz
Ghaemian
Saeid Ghazian Hosein
Ghazi
Nasrullah Ghazizadeh Rahim Kiavar
Taghi Keimanesh Mahdi
Karimi Javad Karimi Naser
Kashkuli
Tahmures Kashkuli Kashani

Kasmaei
Abdullah Kashkuli Alireza
Karimi Naser Kamali Hadik
Ramti Msoud Ganju Hamid
Geramifard Mahdi Geramifard
Firouz Bouran Asad Lalezari
Amid Lashkari
Mahmoud Mahmoudi Nabi Moazami
Reza Malekmohammadi Sohrab Moeini
Ahmad Mohammadi Naser Mahani
Abbas Mokhber Siavash Mirzadeh
Abdullah Mohsen
Kourosh Modarreszadeh Adham
Mohammadzadeh Hosein Madani
Lotfullah Meisami Habid
Mokremdust Ahmad Moeini
Mousa Mohammadnezhad Ahmad mousavi
Mohammad Mozaiian Jamshid Moradian
Jamshid Mohammadzadeh Siamak Mehrsa
Yadullah Madani Badruddin
Madani Ebrahim Mohseni Ali Mir
Riahi Mohammad Milani
Homayoun Mehrani Mohammad
Mousavi
Masha'allah Moftakheri Saei
Moradbakhshi
Amoo Mohammad Kargare Bandarabbas Hosein Mavid
Yousef Mostafavi
Akbar mujeddin Hosein
Mohasel Akbar Masumbeigi
Eskandar Nemati Eidi Nemati
Reza Nematullahi Jahangir
Nematullahi Rasoul Nikpour
Farrokh Negahdar Fazel Namir
Isa Nikkhah Kamran Nakhaei
Farzad Honarpishe

Fazlullah Houshdaran Abbas Hamouni
Masha'allah Helmipour Nader Vahabi
Vakil
Naser Yazdani
List of female political prisoners of Adel Abad
Maryam Pourtangestani Minu
Nematollahi
Azam Kamgouian Sharifeh
Banihashemi Flora Ghadiri
Zohre

LIST OF KILLED PEOPLE IN BUSHEHR

1- Shahpour Mohammad Alipour, who used to work with the Liberation Organization (Nahavandi), in a meeting with one of the members of the Organization, he says that Sirus Nahavandi is suspicious, and shortly after, he disappeared or was killed in 1355(1977).

2- Jamshid Noushzad. The core of the labour-Mahmoud Vahidi-Mohammad Reza Kalntar and Saeed Kord Marachorloo, who was arrested by SAVAK in 1356(1978) and, according to Tehrani's confession, an interrogator of the Joint Committee, was killed by poison and they were related to Jamshid Noshzad. Jamshid Noshzad also died at the end of 1356 (1978) while cleaning his pistol due to an accident with a bullet that hit his throat, and his friends buried his body in one of the deserts around Tehran at night. (Hamneshin Bahar)

Mohammadreza Safarinez, who most probably hid in 1348(1970), and unfortunately, had a sad ending, and the Islamic government executed him.

LIST OF BUSHEHR EXECUTIONS

Akhlaghi, 14 years old Hosein Ande Khideh
Abdullah Ahmadi 1367 Asadi
Bijan Bone Gazi
Hosein Brani 1367
Dariush Borghak 1367 Sabagh
Poursabbagh Mandani Hajipour
Hamidi
Mohammad Dashtaiari Masha'llah
Dashtiari Mokhtar Dorahaki Dorahaki
Mohammad Daraei Gholamreza
Razmju Yadullah Raeisi Abbas
Ravanipour Naser Ranjbar
Ranjbar
Ebrahim Sharifi
Mahdi Sheshboluki 1367 Nasser Shohuli
Hamid Shohuli Hamid Safarinezhad
Mina Talebpour Masha'alah
Tapanche Morteza Gharibi Ahmad
Gharibi Abbas Fakhri
Mahdi Fazel Hasan Fazel
Abdullah Ghaiedi
Kazeruni, 14 years old, Yaghub
Kashefi Kashfi
Seyyed Ali Ganji Gholam Gohari
Mohsen Mosavat Mousavi, 14 years
old Mokhtar Musavi
Enaiatullah Mousavi Mahdi Mohajer
Ebrahim Mohammadian Fazel Namir
1367 Nahid
Ahmad Vaghefi Amir
Hashemi
Jalal Hashemi Tangestani

Lightning Source UK Ltd.
Milton Keynes UK
UKHW011420060122
396705UK00001B/22